A HUCKSTER

FIFTY YEARS ON
THE ROADS OF EUROPE
AND ELSEWHERE

by

Arthur Woods

Published in Great Britain in 2003 by Arthur Woods

Copyright © Arthur Woods, 2003

Designed and typeset by Andrew Haig & Associates

Printed and bound in Great Britain by Antony Rowe Limited

The moral right of the authors has been asserted.

A CIP catalogue record for this book is available from
the British Library.

ISBN 0-9546773-0-7

ACKNOWLEDGEMENTS

It would have been difficult to put this memoir together without the patience and forbearance of my loyal wife In any case her superior spelling and instinctive purity of grammar were absolutely necessary.

Equally, Cindy Foster my secretary for 21 years and the only other person other than my wife who can read my writing, and is as good a speller, made it possible to be written, re-written and typed in 13 weeks. At my age, time, it could be said, is of the essence.

To Michael Legat, novelist, writer and publisher, whose excellent advice on choice of printer and publisher I followed to great advantage.

My sons, Nick and Simon were amused that I should do it, but extremely interested when it was done, and to read many of the stories which had bored them in their youth. If they had a complaint, it was that the parts left out were even more interesting than those put in.

CONTENTS

STARTING OUT

A cloudless day in March 1944 found me lying in a shepherd's hide high on Monte Trocchio, a mountain in Southern Italy 60 miles north of Naples, thinking of what to do with a future for which five years of soldiering had hardly prepared me. On eye level three miles across the valley of the River Liri lay the battered Monastery of Monte Cassino; and in the valley an assortment of soldiers, British, Indian. New Zealanders, and of course, German. 500,000 war weary men; and not an eyelid batted without bringing down on one side or the other artillery bombardment of First World War intensity. Some of which, I'm afraid, was requested by me.

Who would want to employ someone of passing skills in reading a map, directing artillery fire, taking a Lee Enfield or Bren gun apart and re-assembling it? Or even persuading an Arab Bedouin or Italian peasant to part with various goods they swore they hadn't got, such as stolen army kit, guns, and in the case of the Italians, much valued wine? Of course, an officer was supposed to be good at "man management", but in the military circles in which I moved either it was not necessary, or I didn't get the hang of it. Mostly, if there was mutual respect, and everybody knew his job, cockups were easily corrected. It had been from a very early age my strongly held view that cynicism kept you out of trouble; and it was wise to believe only half of what you saw or heard and have strong doubts about the other half. At 83 my disbelief in most things is even stronger.

With the chances of survival reasonable, though by no means certain, I reflected on the foundry industry as a career. Why? Well an old fashioned sector of engineering, redolent of William Blake's dark satanic mills, it might lack for competitors among the modern post war youth.

However, there were a few more rivers to cross and friends to mourn before being chucked out of the army clad in an ill-fitting demob. suit and trilby hat; unprotected from society and having to take decisions which for years the army had done for me.

For two years pre-war I had been serving an indentured mechanical engineering apprenticeship at the old Austin Motor Company, then the largest car manufacturing company outside of the U.S.A. It had many divisions: Design, Manufacturing, Research, Sales, Marketing and Foundry, all of which were open to the student apprentice according to his skills and acceptability So I chose the foundry, the only one to do so among a very mixed bunch which included lieutenants colonel, majors, captains, sergeants and private soldiers, squadron leaders, pilot officers and a fair number of naval officers. They had, without exception, seen it all, disbelieved most of it, were aged from about 24 – 26 going on 40, but with one thing in common, an above average level of intelligence and a willingness to work damned hard for damn little pay, for the remaining 2 years of so of apprenticeship.

The foundry industry, initially anyway, places as great a strain on physical fitness as on the intellect. And to a stranger, (I was not a stranger, having seen it pre-war) it was awesome. If you have never seen liquid iron at 1500 C pouring into a 10 ton ladle swinging from an overhead gantry, guided by a man with little or no protection from either heat or burns, it is terrifying. And to see the same man tilt the ladle with great delicacy so that its lip discharges molten iron into quite a small hole in a sand mould seems heroic.

I can think of only one profession older than the foundry and both, in the right hands, are highly profitable. Even if, in the case of the foundry, highly taxed, as all industry was under the Labour Government of 1945/52, and, of course, later under Wilson, Callaghan et al. But I remember reading a piece of wisdom written by a 17th century ironmaster:

Iron seemeth a simple metal
But in its nature are many mysteries.
And men that bend them to their minds
Shall, in arriving Days

Gather therefrom great profit,
Not for them alone, but for all mankind.

So why not give it a go?

The Austin Motor Co was built (and still remains under the name of Rover) on the outskirts of Birmingham, and drew its labour force of some 60,000 from all of the West Midlands. In the case of the iron, and also the steel foundry, most of the workers both male and female came from the Black Country towns and villages of Lye, Cradley Heath, Halesowen, Tipton and Stourbridge, among many others. Also the Worcestershire villages of:

Upton, Snodsbury, Pershore, Crole,
North Piddle, Wyre Piddle, Piddle-in-the-Hole."

Travelling was usually by an excellent train service direct to the works.. These places had been the source of metal working since the Middle Ages, particularly since the 17th century when the demands of the Industrial Revolution brought the farm labourers out of the fields and into the manufactories, frequently based on the small houses in the villages which became the places for making chains, horse shoes, iron balls and a variety of small tools, made by forging and hammering billets of iron heated in a crude coke fired furnace. These were the people from whom were drawn the foundry workers of the 19th and 20th centuries to make the variety of castings in iron, steel, aluminium, brass and bronze to feed every industry under the sun in Birmingham, the greatest industrial centre of the 19th century.

And a rough lot they were too. Uneducated but not unlettered., they could write a letter that today seems to be beyond their successors in the work place. In 1946 little had changed since 1939 except that the unions, flushed with war time victories had assumed such arrogance that they called the tune to which management danced unless they wanted (always unofficial, of course) a strike that would shut a plant down. I recall a shop steward who boasted that he could stop production over the quality of the canteen tea – and he did. Hardly a week went by without a stoppage on the most trivial excuse. It was such naked exhibition of union power that was the main cause of the collapse of the UK as an industrial power by 1982. It saw the destruction of the motor bike industry, the cycle industry, the machine tool industry, and, worst of all, the motor car industry. In 1954 we were the biggest exporters of motor cars in Europe. By 1980 our total production was hardly that of Spain, and we imported over 70% of our cars, as the total of days lost to strikes exceeded 10 million annually.

The industrial unrest was rather less apparent within the foundry than in the other Austin workshops. Somehow the union officials found the atmosphere of the foundry arcane and difficult to understand and organise. So, to a large extent they escaped the worst of the disruptions. Arcane, indeed; only in the foundry would you have seen the furnace man asleep after his breakfast at 7 o'clock on a bag of sand. And only in the foundry would you have seen said furnace man waking up to see a pair of dead red eyed rats on his chest about 6 inches from his face. Placed there by his friends of course.

Then there were the coreshop girls; more foul mouthed and lewd than the men. In the coreshop sand shapes were made which hollowed out the castings. There was a famous incident during the war, possibly apocryphal but there were those who swore to its authenticity, when a cheeky 16 year old boy had his trousers removed, an iron ring placed on his penis which one of the girls roused to an excited hardness. The story stops at that point. Let it be said you learned more in the foundry about life in the raw than a bank clerk.

Early in 1949 I parted from Austin having decided it best to part from my place of training, and I was with several companies working at the high tec end of the foundry industry. However it seemed likely that my talents, such as they were, lay in the direction of developing of ideas and marketing without the restrictions imposed by large structured organisations. In short, I was not a true company man. One day in January 1952, idly scanning the small ads in the Daily Telegraph, a paper I read only occasionally, a job advertisement caught my eye. Now, it is usually the smallest of things which start a train of events which can change your life for better, or perhaps worse. This ad turned out to be such, and it read:

An engineering group, London based, requires an engineer of metallurgical and foundry training to work as Personal Assistant to the Managing Director of its foundry division.

I answered it, received a reply requiring my attendance for an interview at the Grosvenor Hotel, and so I went along. A Sloane Ranger type secretary ushered me into an elegant suite and a tall, amiable man came to see me, and explain a thing or two. "Lord Trefgarne will see you, although he says the situation may already have been offered to another applicant". "Lord Trefgarne" I thought, "I've heard that name somewhere." I waited another twenty minutes, delving into the recesses of my memory, and then it came to me. He was a Labour peer, ennobled in 1945 when the Labour Party came to power, involved in one or two crackpot socialist schemes which came to nought but cost millions. Later on I learnt more about this quite extraordinary man. He was formerly George Garro-Jones, a barrister, a Liberal M.P. and a First World War pilot in the Royal Flying Corps. In 1931 Ramsay MacDonald, the first ever Labour Prime Minister voted in 1929, formed a National Government with the Tory Party, from which it never recovered until 1945. Garro-Jones, showing extraordinary political acuteness, left the Liberals and joined the Labour Party which was in crisis, for which he was duly rewarded in 1945. This small, quiet man of penetrating intellect quickly put me at ease, explaining he was exploiting a revolutionary foundry idea called the Croning Process, after its German inventor, Johannes Croning. "You probably haven't heard of it, he said. But I had. In late 1946 I recalled reading a short article in a trade journal about something called the McKellar Report. It dealt briefly with a Committee named "The Custodian of Enemy Property" which during a visit to Germany discovered a revolutionary foundry development called The Croning Process.

I quoted this McKellar Report verbatim to Trefgarne. Had the term been in use in 1952 he could have been described as "gobsmacked". There was an unnerving silence of about 30 seconds, then he said "You can have the job, Mr. Woods, if you want".

Once again Trefgarne, while heading this Committee, had displayed his intuitive skill in recognising a complicated technical process that could be exploited, though he had no foundry or engineering knowledge. He was also the owner and chief shareholder of the largest manufacturer of gears and gear boxes in the UK and I was to work for him for five years, continuing the further development of the "C" Process as it came to be called in the Anglo-Saxon countries and selling it under license to a wide variety of foundries, Trefgarne having done a private deal with Johannes Croning to exploit the Process in the UK and other countries.

Here began my European and other wanderings.

A PASSAGE TO INDIA

I WAS UNHAPPY WHEN I HAD NO SHOES,

UNTIL I MET A MAN WHO HAD NO FEET

August 1952 found me preparing for my first major job for Lord Trefgarne, Always an expansionist and an internationalist, he chose India as the first overseas country in which to test the water with our revolutionary foundry process. But there was a sound reason for choosing India. His Personal Assistant Ward Morden, had worked in India before the second World War, remained there during the war and for several years after. He was in fact, in the jargon of the time an "old India hand", with wide knowledge of the sub-continent both geographical and personal through a network of business associates. The Raj since the time of Clive of India, mid eighteenth century, had established a system of trading like no other on earth. It was not started by conquest, that came later, but by the Honourable East India Company in the seventeenth century, generally known as John Company, who even established their own army, and which remained intact until the Mutiny of 1857. After which, India became ruled from London, and the Indian Army was established; also controlled from London by the War Office.

After the Mutiny trading settled down into an extraordinary structure based largely on the Managing Agents, operating hands on in India but with London Headquarters. What was it that drove so many Scotsmen abroad? The weather – yes, the food such as it was (and that was before the deep fried Mars bar) – yes. The gloom laden Calvinistic religions in which you could fornicate on a Sunday but not whistle? Well, why not. The Managing Agents were full of them, and history showed that, in the words of P.G. Wodehouse "Nothing is so awesome as observing a Scotsman on the make", and make it they did. One such Agent was Andrew Yule, well established since before the Mutiny and, even in 1952, they still managed a large slice of the coal mines, iron ore, steel industries and tex-tiles.

Now Ward Morden, an Anglo Canadian, had joined Andrew Yule in 1935 at the age of 21. Quickly, after he landed at Calcutta, and despite his lowly status, he found himself "A ruler amid the ruled". That was India, hardly changed since pre-Edwardian days as far as present relationships with the Hindus were concerned. Unmarried, he lived in a "chummery" with six or more other clerks. This was a large bungalow equipped with at least the minimum of comfort that a European expected in India, large bedroom, sittingroom, bathroom, billiards room cook and personal servant. All this was way beyond the salary of a young man starting on his career. But it was normal and approved by Yule, indeed the company planned it that way. Debt was managed, within reason, and why? Because, said Morden, you were promised such wealth in your last three years with the company that at 50, it would pay all debts and allow you to retire home, buy a small estate with perhaps a Georgian country house and an extremely comfortable pension income. Morden had another in-teresting link with India. There is a great industrial trading family called Tata, who, though big in 1936 have grown mightily since. In 1926, Ward Morden's father, a noted early aviator in Canada, came to India and taught J.R. Tata, the then head of Tata, to fly. The Tata's are Parsees, of that extraordinary sect the Zoroastrians who pre-date Christianity by a couple of thousand years. They came from Persia, mostly to avoid the Moslems who conquered Persia in about 670 A.D., and settled in the Bombay area. An intelligent, cultured race it gradually established consid-erable authority particularly in the field of commerce. Not generally known about in the U.K., except for the practice of placing their dead on flat topped wooden towers to be picked clean by vultures. The Towers of Silence, as they are called, are an extremely hygienic practice in a hot country.

On the outbreak of war in September 1939 Ward, like most of the ex-pats, joined up; in the Rajputana Rifles. For a period of a year or so towards the end of the war in Burma he was seconded from the Indian Army to be the Commander of the Rajah of Jodphur's private army back in the State of Jodphur. "Avery nice numero", he said, with many benefits in kind generally not available to your average infantry officer; even the eccentric morning duty of joining the Rajah on the double throned lavatory. It provided the opportunity of discussing the day's affairs informally.

The major U.K. airline from 1947 was BOAC (British Overseas Airline Corporation) and it flew the long haul routes worldwide except to South American countries, for another nationalised air line, British South American, did that. BOAC was housed in a series of Nissan huts, those strange pre-fabricated structures with a semi-circular roof. Very comfortable, positively genteel; only the very privileged flew in those days and the planes were staffed by well educated girls, the Sloane Rangers of the period. Each passenger was given a blue shoulder bag with BOAC on it, and was much prized at the time as visible evidence that its owner had actually flown overseas. It had the cachet of a television aerial in the 50's, and even today some old bloke is to be seen carrying one; probably full of his dirty laundry en route to a washarama.

The destination was Bombay, an awesome 6,000 mile flight and was to take about 23 hours. The plane, I think, was a 4-engined DC6, which was top wing giving the impression, almost, of sitting on the ground. The seating, in retrospect, is remembered as quite generous and the food O.K. But certain things are memorable; the landing in Rome by moonlight just after flying low over St. Peter's basilica, and an absolutely empty Piazza. Coming out of the plane in Cyprus, Nicosia, to be hit in the face by an African heat I had not felt since wartime in Egypt. Then flying high over Crete, probably at 10,000 feet, yet the dark,brooding mountains seemed close enough to touch. Early the same evening we landed at Bahrein on the simplest of airfields with all wooden buildings. A lot of people waited alongside the airstrip, not so much to meet passengers as to meet the plane; it was an event that happened once every day; the plane from home to be greeted by the ex-pats eager for newspapers and talk from home. 4,000 miles from home in those days in isolation terms was more than 20,000 today One irritation we are spared today is the short bulletin coming from the flight deck which you were expected to read and pass to the passengers behind you. Worse was to come, the pilot would leave his steering wheel or joystick or whatever it was called and walk down the gangway glad handing everybody. A train driver was not expected to do that, so why a pilot? Today of course it has been replaced by something even worse; the celebrity chef emerging from the restaurant kitchen to mingle with the craven clients who are expected to praise his food even if you thought it tasted like dog shit. Karachi in the late evening and then Bombay in the morning, 23 hours after leaving Heath Row – and it felt like it!

Bombay with a shade temperature of 90F and a humidity of 98 leaves you feeling weak, and to deal with it requires you to walk with a slow, measured step. Our hotel was not the Taj Mahal, though we could see it from our neat, modest lodging, and later we stayed there. Built in the 19th century it had all the splendour and grandeur of the European Grand Hotels of London, Paris, Rome and Venice, though with many more servants. But first things first, we had to find our shipping agent and get him to the "go-down" in the dock area to check that all our kit had arrived, having been shipped 3 months earlier. A "go-down" is the Anglo Indian term for a warehouse, but why?, nobody could explain, certainly not Ward Morden who had been using the term for nearly 20 years. What he *had* forgotten was that Bombay and the State of Gujerat was "dry" by order of Desai the puritanical and tee-total Governor, said to have been appointed by Nehru as a joke on the British. A sort of old Harovian joke. No matter, as always in India things are never what they seem. Whisky was regarded as a medicine and an obliging doctor was readily available to write a prescription for a European (not for an Indian) for a bottle of scotch, or gin, or brandy per week. Then I was taught by Ward how to drink scotch in India. You take a tumbler, put in two fingers of whisky and fill to the brim with water. That gives you a chotta peg, three fingers and it becomes a bura peg. By all accounts a drink so made is no less alcoholic than straight liquor but it avoids dehydration. I must say that, within an hour of entering our hotel the scotch was safely in our hands. India was, and still is, a country in the hands of the bureaucrats but where drink for the European is concerned they relented with commendable wisdom. So that evening, each with a bura peg taken, we started slowly, gently to mingle with a never ending, moving mass of humanity which was, and is, the same in any town, Hindu or Moslem, in India. Noisy, squalid, unsightly beggars sans legs, sans arms, sans arms *and* legs; yet all seemed to be receiving alms, a pice perhaps, an anna, or even a rupee. We went to a tailor of Ward's acquaintance who measured me for another tropical suit which he promised would be made and delivered to the hotel in 24 hours. Then to bed but not to sleep. Jet lag or whatever it is called when travelling East rather than West for 23 hours prevented sleep. So every hour or so I looked out of the window and always there was a slow moving crowd and, I suppose, the second shift of mendicants. I have been surprised in recent years when talking to people about my work that most did not know what a foundry is. The Oxford dictionary describes it as the place where metal is cast into moulds (1601A.D.) For the layman I don't think that is enough. The practice certainly dates back at least 5,000 years and probably further. The original principal despite such a passage of time remains much the same. If, say, in 2,000 B.C. it was required to make a bar of brass about six feet long with a two inch diameter, you would first fashion a stave out of wood of the required size. Then you would lay it down on a bed of clay, cover it entirely in clay and then withdraw the stave leaving behind the cavity it had occupied. You have now made a mould and molten metal can then be poured (cast) in at one end. If only it was as simple as that but the making of a casting in a foundry consists of making a mould and filling it with iron or steel, brass or aluminium or one of many other metals. Look at the engine in a car. You will see a cylinder head, a motor block and inside that is a crankshaft, a camshaft, a water pump and other smaller castings, all made in a foundry. And the processes by which they are made are many.

The overall purpose of the business trip was to review the Indian foundry industry (not Pakistan) and determine where our foundry "C" process had application. We had, of course, done plenty of research in the U.K. on Indian industry for several months before departure, and made contact with many large companies at the highest level. That was Ward's job.

To carry out demonstrations and lecture on the foundry practice and metallurgy involved, and the gains, technological and commercial, to be expected. That was my job. Ward had used his contacts, old boy network, etc, especially his old employer the Managing Agents, Andrew

Yule. Resulting from which demonstration centres in both Bombay and Calcutta were granted to us, so that groups of interested parties could attend. It would not have been practical to give demonstrations in individual foundries, too much in the way of equipment or materials was involved.

But before commencing we visited the works of the interested parties to examine their suitability as practitioners of the "C" process. Most, at their level of sophistication, were not, although over the next twenty years or so many of them became users. As indeed did the rest of the industrial world. In 1952 there were perhaps 50 foundries in Western Europe and the U.S.A. using the "C" process. As I write it is over 5,500 and twenty years ago, before the considerable diminution of the world's industrial base, twice that number.

Three great advantages were offered, weight reduction, accuracy and a reduction of labour content. With teeming millions of workers at low pay rates that ruled out India. I remember some years previously speaking with a very experienced engineer who had been invited b y the Indian Government of the day to build a fully automated foundry, and to decide which product to cast. He came out with no pre-conceived ideas as to what could be produced. Then he saw the perfect application – brass rice bowls which were used in their tens of millions. He rubbed his hands over this, until he examined costs. To his disbelief he discovered that a bowl could be bought at less than the cost of the brass of which it was made. They were made in very small foundries employing only a handful of men, and the brass which was melted to make them was mostly stolen. Of the considerable number of people met in Bombay I was surprised by the small number of Europeans encountered in the foundry industry, indeed in any industry.

So it was largely structured from top to bottom by local people, and they were an absolute delight with a high level of education. Bombay had not much to recommend it although it had been British since the 1660's, coming as it did to Charles the Second as part of the dowry of his Portuguese wife, Catherine of Braganza.

After four weeks and what, on the face of it, was a very promising start, and glad not to have been killed in one of the many Sikh driven taxis, our normal transport, we left to go to Calcutta on the night train.

An air conditioned coupé, opulent, well servanted and the route used by the many servants of the Raj for nearly 100 years. Generals, Rajahs, Maharajahs and members of the I.C.S. (the Indian Civil Service), the crème de la crème of the British Civil Service, had all travelled on this train regularly and in an air conditioned coupé.

Now that was an experience and for those who saw the film Bhowani Junction, from the book by John Masters, himself a very old India hand and a long serving officer in the Ghurkas will know what I mean. The chaos, the crowds, the noise, the fight for seats (though not for us), the summoning of servants by high caste Indians koi hai (is anybody there?). And then the departure with as many people on top of the train as inside it. It was not an interesting journey across featureless plains, as seen in daylight, but comfortable and cool with much food and drink served before bed. Of greater interest were the halts at some stations where, during the half hour pause, food and drink were rushed along the platform by a horde of vendors, and trade was brisk.

A pleasing feature often seen in the streets and also from the train was that of young boys playing cricket, bare footed and with the most primitive bats and wickets, with such shouts of joy that I have not heard in the home of cricket these 50 years. It may explain why we produce few great players these days but India, with Pakistan, do by the score.

Calcutta at last, in the afternoon of the following day. Larger, smellier, with more beggars, thousands living on the pavements, but full of beautiful buildings, private as well as public; examples of Victorian architecture and also Georgian. Government House was built in 1800 and when Lord Curzon arrived as Viceroy in 1899 he felt very much at home since its plan was based on his house, Kedleston Hall in Derbyshire. A feature still in place were the nearly six foot high Indian storks perched on the top.

Our hotel, a good one, was on Chowringhee, a great centre of opulence where lived the big swinging dicks of the Civil Service, Magistrates and high servants of the Raj up until Partition in 1947, still occupied by the same professions but mostly Indian now not British. The Bengal Club of 1827 is there, but the only Bengalis allowed in were servants, except for the odd Rajah or two. Ward still had friends among the members and we were to dine at the Club before leaving India.

Our business here was to be a replica of Bombay. Ward had obtained the use of the foundry laboratory belonging to the Indian Iron and Steel Company, owned, of course, by Andrew Yule. A meeting had been arranged at the office of Andrew Yule for 8 the next morning, a short walk along from our hotel, and we arrived at about 07.45. There was no-one about and so we walked into the large general office completely empty of people but full of about 50 small desks, each with a ledger on its sloping top, and a stool in front of it. Clearly these desks were waiting for the clerks (babus) to arrive. Ward had seen this many times but I had not and I had the insane idea of changing the ledgers around to confuse the poor babus when they arrived. I did not – it would have been very cruel

The foundry was about ten miles to the north of the city, and with it as our operational centre we carried out demonstrations, gave lectures and arranged visits to foundries and companies over a range of 50 miles from the city centre. The monsoons were only a week or two away, and the weather reflected their nearness. The skies were overcast, but temperatures were in th nineties and humidity required at least three shirt changes daily. Sometimes the sun in late afternoon would break through and it was pleasant to sit in the pavilion of the Calcutta Cricket Club watching a match, cool drink in hand and listening to a mixture of knowledgeable cricket chat, business chit-chat and the sadness of older members, some with thirty years of India under their belts. They found it difficult to come to terms with the relative loss of authority since Partition. Yet the wise among them had seen it coming since 1918 and had come to accept the inevitability. Here they were, nearing their last plane or boat trip home, reflecting on how thirty thousand civil servants and never more than seventy thousand soldiers had administered a population of Hindus, Muslims, Sikhs and dozens of religious sects, totalling more than five hundred million. In Ireland, during the unrest of 1916/1920, there were more than seventy thousand troops to police a population of only two and a half millions.

One day I was strolling, very slowly, sweating buckets and looking in the bazaars; carefully avoiding the cows and goats and throwing an anna or two into outstretched hands or tin mugs. I was looking for a piece of ivory much made in Kashmir consisting of a number of balls, perhaps 5, each contained within another so that from the outer ball of about three and a half inches diameter could be seen the inner balls down to one inch diameter, each ball exquisitely carved. How it was carved and assembled with no apparent joins I could not imagine. On the pavement, just as I was about to enter a shop I caught the eye of a man, and he saw and recognised me at the same instant. It was Chandra Roy, an Austin apprentice at the same time as me, l946 onwards. We had been quite friendly but I had not known then that his family owned the concession for the distribution and sale of Austin cars and vehicles in Bengal and Bihar – big business. It was a chance meeting and a pleasant one, and when he heard what I was looking for he offered his local knowledge to get the best at the lowest price. So I left it to him. Anyway, we saw each other several times in the next few days, although he had not yet found the ivory balls. "But don't worry" he said "I shall have it tomorrow and will bring it to your hotel." Well, he did not turn up and the next day I phoned his office "Mr Roy is sick but he should be about tomorrow." Two days later I phoned again and was told "Mr Roy is still poorly, but should be up and about in a few days." Well, he never did turn up and I never saw him again. When I told the story to Ward Morden he said "I am not surprised. He failed to get what he had promised and suffered such loss of face he felt he couldn't meet you." He may have been right and it was certainly something I had never encountered before. Anyway, I found what I wanted at a disgustingly low price. India is not Europe – but then, why should it be?

Towards the end of our Calcutta stay Ward said we were both invited as guests of Bill Cato (later Lord Cato), Chief Executive of Andrew Yule at the Bengal Club. Ward promised me a memorable evening which I would not forget for a very long time. About twenty of us sat down, we being the only guests, the others being club members, some with their Memsahibs. I had long heard of the formidable women in India but this was the first time we were to meet.

It was a long panelled room, brilliantly lit by massive chandeliers which filled every corner with light to do justice to the portraits of 18th century grandees, 19th and 20th century taipans (heads) of the Honourable East Indian Company, Viceroys of the Raj and an assortment of the great and the good, who for better or for worse had ruled most of the Indian sub-continent since the days of Clive in the mid 18th century.

It would have been surprising had they not been critical of the 1947 Partition which broke India into three parts: Hindu India generally in the centre with a population of some 450 millions; Muslim India renamed Pakistan in the North West and, 2,000 miles to the South East adjacent to Bengal Calcutta, East Pakistan later renamed Bangladesh. The Muslim people totalled about 80 millions. Today, of course, all those figures have doubled those of 1947. They were savagely bitter about Earl Mountbatten, the last Viceroy, and the speed (in their view indecent haste) with which he pushed through Partition, causing over a million dead in the four weeks that millions were on the move relocating themselves, sometimes over many hundreds of miles. There were communal riots in which neighbour murdered neighbour with barbarism and atrocities of awesome magnitude. The knife was the preferred weapon of use and throat cutting, women and children especially, the usual method of despatch. That apart, the conversation and wit, rich in gallows humour, was exhilarating and sometimes hilarious, based as it was on the wisdom of experience and, sometimes, fear when disease struck with lightning speed, killing with undiscriminating carelessness, men, women and children – but especially children. If you were the third, fourth or even fifth generation to have worked in India, believe me, you had plenty to talk about. As for the Memsahibs, the suffering wives, their conversation was rich on servants (lazy, dishonest), babus (cheeky, half-educated), shopkeepers (dishonest, filthy), Hindu politicians (rabble rousers, communists, dishonest, over-educated). You could have been a guest in the Tory Carlton Club, but to hear it 6,000 miles gave it an extra edge.

While the conversation flowed we were served food of Lucullan splendour and richness and I doubt if that Roman ever supped better. Behind each guest was a turbanned servant, clad in white with collars, cuffs and waist edged in gold and crimson. While huge punkahs on the high ceiling turned silently but effectively we ate magnificently of English and French cooking and French wines to be dreamt of. Certainly such fare had never come my way before and only rarely since. The courses and wines I never forgot, and frequently over the years I think fondly on:

Crab Consommé served with Fino La Ina sherry
Poached Salmon (from Simla) served with Krug champagne 1945
Saddle of Lamb served with Chateau Margaud 1937
Stilton Cheese served with Cockburn Port 1920
Chocolate Souffle served with Chateau Yquem 1936

And the streets of Calcutta, 2 minutes from us, were packed with the poor, many of whom thought themselves fortunate to have a bowl of rice a day. Even Christ as he was saying "The poor are always with us" could not have imagined the starving masses in the India of his day.

So, what lay behind this end product of such opulence? Well, you could say tea production for the English and other markets, hemp for the Dundee trade perhaps. But you would have been wrong; it was opium, the product of the beautiful, insidious poppy. It all began with the Honourable East India Company which was granted the monopoly of Indian trade by Elizabeth the First in 1600. This they held through Clive of India up to and beyond the Mutiny of 1857, and for general trade more or less until 1900. In the late 18th century they encountered the opium poppy freely growing in Bengal with its stupefying effect and granting of a temporary Nirvana to those who smoked it. This, they quickly grasped, was better than the Philosopher's Stone. Cheap labour, low cost product, a ready market in China, 1,000 per cent profit and Bingo! This was like winning a national lottery jackpot every week. So they organised the small farmers on hundreds of thousands of acres to grow the poppy in a well organised, well disciplined Anglo Saxon (or maybe Scottish) manner. The juice from the poppy heads was then sent as a viscous resin to the factory in Patna or Benares where processing turned it into balls about the size of a man's head. These were then sold by the Government of India at 40 heads per chest to be sold by public auction in Calcutta and from whence they went forth upon their mission of soothing John Chinaman into a temporary forgetfulness.

Now at this point it must be said that the Government in London regarded the trade as illegal and so did the Indian Government and so also did the Manchu Government living in dreamy isolation in Peking, thousands of miles from the action, which was in Canton and Macao. But all three of them were in on the take. Only the East India Company were honest in a dishonest sort of way, and just got with the business of selling the opium. Then in 1831 everything changed. Then John Company, as the H.E.L. Co. were called, lost the monopoly of Indian trade (London just took it off them), and the world moved in on the opium trade, but mostly two Scotsmen, William Jardine, a surgeon well established in Calcutta, and Sir James Matheson, a Scottish baronet who worked in Canton, together they formed Jardine and Matheson Ltd which eventually controlled the larger part of the opium game. Jardine even had built three 20 gun frigates, fast vessels which the Royal Navy envied, to protect the opium clippers against Chinese pirates as they sailed to do the selling to the Chinese Government middle men at Macao and Canton. Later Jardine & Matheson decided to cut our the middle men and sailed the South China seas to sell direct in the smaller ports. Willing sellers – willing buyers; Capitalism red in tooth and claw. The American's admiration was unbounded for such Protestant enterprise. Lest you have forgotten, this was all illegal. However, this was not enough. The British Government, still ashamed at their involvement, wanted to supplant, or at least add to, its own burgeoning manufactured goods. For, after defeating the French and Napoleon, Great Britain was the greatest country and greatest manufacturer in the world. And as the U.S.A. was later to flex its industrial muscles, wanted China to open all its ports to legitimate trade. The Chinese Government would have none of it. It regarded the British, indeed all non-Chinese, as savage, ill-mannered barbarians to whom they would sell silk and tea, while buying opium, or "Foreign Mud" as they called it at arm's length, while metaphorically holding fingers to noses. No foreigners were to penetrate beyond the outside of Canton's walls. Then things started to get a bit rough. A confiscation of 20,000 chests of opium at Canton, humiliation of British merchants and so on. Finally a suitable casus belli was seized on by the British Government to declare war on the Chinese and after a couple of naval engagements in 1840 a Chinese fleet was demolished and by the Treaty of Nanking, six Treaty ports from Canton northwards to Shanghai were granted to the British, along with Hong Kong. The opium trade continued at a much higher level and did not finish until 1908. Messrs. Jardine and Matheson, among many others, died hugely wealthy on their grand estates in the U.K., and Jardine Matheson are still strong today.

The British Government, while despising the opium trade, made no great effort to end it. The tax revenue was so huge it played a major role in industrial and civil development in India. When it was finally banned it was too late. History may yet consider how serious was the role played by the British in developing the world's present craving for drugs in not clamping down on the opium trade much earlier.

Up until 1908 opium was legally and widely available from any chemist in the U.K. So it can be said, I suppose that it was the opium trade, and all the wealth it had garnered for individuals, companies and governments, that made it possible for me to take dinner in September 1957 amongst great splendour

It was now time to leave India. In October after ten weeks amidst filth, splendour and exotic surroundings we penetrated a very difficult market which, over the years to follow, yielded great profit. We journeyed back to Bombay by train, but not in an air conditioned coupé. It was a two-berth but without air conditioning. In fact, except for being alone in our compartment, we were as uncomfortable as those in third class, and definitely hotter than the hundreds of non paying passengers travelling on the roof. It was not only the heat, which topped 100.F, but the dust. There was no glass on the door but a fine mesh gauze through which a finer dust entered. After a short while we stripped down to our underpants which gave some respite. Bombay, twentyfour hours later, was like emerging from a coal pit, and the Taj Mahal hotel was like entering the Islamic Paradise, though without the feminine consolation.

A great surprise awaited us at Karachi Airport where we flew from Bombay the next day. We boarded the Comet airplane which flew daily from London. It was the first jet engined passenger plane to fly commercially and was a world sensation, reducing long haul flights by nearly a half, though with the same refueling stops. It had, I think, only been in service for a year.

Take off was startling, not the gentle build up of speed as on a piston engined plane, but a violent thrust that pushed you back in your seat. Thirteen hours later we landed at Heathrow. For those who remember the Comet, and it still flies militarily, there were accidents to the three in service. Ours was the first accident; it went down to the bottom of the sea off the coast of Sicily six months later. "Metal fatigue" they said.

SPAIN AND PORTUGAL

AS FLIES TO WANTON BOYS ARE WE TO THE GODS

THEY KILL US FOR THEIR SPORT

No war is worse than Civil War. It is cruel, unforgiving, savage; obeying no rules. Forget the Geneva Convention, it divides families, communities, sometimes putting son against father, sister against mother. Everything that is bad in civil war found a role in Spain between 1936 and 1939, and the Gods did indeed kill people for their sport. The hatred continued remorselessly after Franco and his fascist regime triumphed and began the years of condign punishment against the defeated Republican ragtaggle force of Socialists, Communists, Anarchists and the International Brigade who travelled to Spain, on foot, without pay, without weapons, no uniforms and, frankly, no ideas on how to fight against a well armed conventional army. They went, as they thought, to defend democracy against fascism. But it is as wrong to be too early with a good idea s it is to be too late. These defenders of democracy were too early and were referred to scornfully as premature anti-fascists when they returned (less the 25% who were killed) to the U.K., the U.S.A., Italy, France and other places. 500,000 Spaniards are said to have been killed which, if accurate, the proven arithmetic of war puts the wounded at three times that number. What a butcher's bill. I recall a young Englishman, held in a Madrid prison, who witnessed daily from his cell window Spaniards being executed with the garrotte, a most painful form of strangulation.

It was the May of 1953 at 6pm when I drove through the open jaws of the British Rail ferry Lord Warden at Dover. The weather was tranquil, pleasant and the roadside covered in wild flowers, for this was 1953 remember. If I had thought of it at the time I would have been murmuring the line, "Where ignorance is bliss, 'tis folly to be wise", for I was about to jump into the deep end without anybody to tell me I should have learnt how to swim first.

However, I had 600 miles of French roads to complete before crossing into Spain at Irun, the Franco-Spanish border on the Bay of Biscay, and I intended to make the most of it in food, drink and all the other things that had contributed to my love/hatred for France and all things French.

At that time, and for many years after at least until about 1965 when it was de-nationalised, British Rail ran what must have been the most inefficient and most expensive ferry service in Europe and still lost money. Even when a modicum of opposition was allowed it was false competition, since the prices were always the same to the penny. There was a shipping line called Townsend-Thorensen and I remember, in a foul mood, writing a hugely insulting letter to the owner of Townsend-Thorensen. It was posted before my wife could read it and tear it up and she usually did with such letters. To my surprise, on what must have been the day the letter reached his desk, he dropped down dead. I often wondered if it was after reading my acrid prose.

Calais was a small run-down town, cobbled throughout with the dreaded French pavé, which was to be my constant tormentor for the next 16 years. In 1968 the students' revolt in Paris, against De Gaulle, the lads and their many supporters from abroad discovered the cobble to be a handy and available weapon against the police. A twist with a knife quickly released a lethal missile from the ground for throwing, and in plentiful supply. So it took the student revolution to improve the French roads; for in no time at all the pavé came up and the asphalt went down.

Calais, though a town of historical significance, seemed to offer little to the traveller. As I later discovered, hotels were shabby, unclean and unwelcoming. Then, few British with cars came over except at holiday time. Yet the nearness to Dover should have had greater influence. The short leap of 26 miles to the U.K. seemed to increase the difference between the nations rather than to bring them closer. A simple thing like a cup of tea; how could the French not master the small task of making a reasonable cup of tea? The Swiss 400 miles away had no problem. But the French! Hot milk, tepid water, weak and with not even the choice of lemon. It had to be deliberate. But then, the coffee was lousy, unless you liked chicory, so why should the tea be any better? Pour encourager les Anglais? Not bloody likely. The shame of 1940's capitulation, and the worse shame of rescue by the British and the Americans in 1944 was a point not laboured upon in 1950/1960 France.

So for the open road. Blue sky, little cloud, warmish, little traffic. I felt like Mr. Toad, parp parp! Down the N1, Boulogne, Montreuil, Abbeville, still showing its wartime battering. No by-pass, so France through the centuries was seen and the narrow streets of medieval Picardy were crossed, the air full of smells new to my nostrils (well, fairly new) of breakfast coffee, fresh bread and the early morning Gitane and Gaulois cigarettes, those world leaders in the coffin nail competition. Rather slower through Rouen because of the river, slow enough to observe the Place de Cathèdrale where the English burnt Joan of Arc in 1431. A lesson to be learned in those turbulent days, if a woman ever upset the men *and* the Church at the same time, that really was asking for it.

On to Chartres, Tours, across the Loire, still on N10, Poitiers, where once again the English long bow triumphed over the French crossbow in 1456. Roads now quite empty and so on to Angoulême and then Bordeaux, which I by-passed, to go a little way up the River Dordogne and find the village of St.Emilion which, along with the Medoc a few miles north of Bordeaux, produced the greatest red wine in the whole of the world. That had been my destination from the moment I crossed onto French soil, and the reason I didn't stop for lunch. 530 miles and 9 hours later, I sat down to a fine spread and wines to dream about that only rustic France in those days could provide. Not stopping for lunch and so eating only early morning and evening was the pattern I followed for the next forty years when motoring the roads of Europe

Next morning I drove through the narrow twisting roads that lay between St. Emilion, the hills of the latter, along with those of Pomerol were covered with low growing vines pruned in the Guyot system, which is the basic method of viticulture in Bordeaux, giving low yields but intense, concentrated quality. I got out to have a closer look and saw that the buds were swelling, ready to burst into leaf in a day or two. Soon I met the main road going South from Bordeaux, straight and fast, through few villages but many pine forests on sandy soil. Large metal cups attached to some of the pines were a puzzle, until I realised the trees had been tapped, and the cups were collecting the resin. Biarritz was quickly reached, and easy to drive through, a delightful aristocratic Summer resort, much patronised by the English especially in Edwardian times, but still visited by the better breeched middle classes. Then a few lovely yachting villages, especially St.-Jean-de-Luz, before the border at Hendaye/Irun. I could see Spain but was not yet in it.

There were sturdy barriers at the crossing point, not as in democratic Western European countries where there were no physical barriers, just Customs Officials barring the way. Entrance to Spain was much the same, as I was to find out later, as into the countries of Eastern Europe, client states of the U.S.S.R. Armed police, armed soldiers and sinister men in cheap suits. Fascism of the Left and of the Right have much in common. Delay in such circumstances is part of the game and, it helps to justify their existence, for the tasks they had to perform could have been done by two or three people rather than the dozen or more milling around. No English was spoken here, and not much French which was surprising. Despite my Spanish, more or less limited to "hasta la vista",and "cerveza" (it is always useful when in a strange country to know the word for beer), I was through Customs

and away in not much more than an hour. Bilbao, my destination, was about 60m miles West on the coast. Through San Sebastian, another elegant town not unlike Cannes or Nice, and about ten miles West was a small village on a very sharp bend. The road though poor was clear and the houses were not visible until the bend was entered, at which point its dangerous nature was not apparent. I just about got round it without sliding into a large pond on the right. Later, a couple of years later, I passed that way on a Sunday Afternoon, rather more sedately, and saw a small crowd gathered on the left opposite the pond. Out of interest I stopped and asked why the crowd. A chap laughed and said "It's the French". "What do you mean?" I asked, "Well, every Sunday they come into Spain for a spin, driving as the French do, go too fast into the bend, and every now and then one of them gets dunked in the pond. We always come out on Sunday to watch." There were not too many laughs in Spain in those days, especially in this Basque Province. The Basque people of the Province of Viscaya, fiercely independent, opposed Franco more than any other part of Spain and were punished accordingly, deprivation of Government grants, severe local laws, over-policed, etc. Catalonia with its capital of Barcelona suffered much the same and for the same reasons yet, ironically, both Viscaya and Catalonia were the most industrially developed areas of the country, and earned most of the much needed foreign currency. Centred on Bilbao was a thriving foundry industry and I had made contact with a small family firm who had for several generations been prominent in the sale of equipment and materials to the Spanish trade. Iloduya e Cia was to be my company's Spanish agent for many years, and the sons, who were many, and a plentiful supply of daughters plus Señor and Señora Iloduya were my friends for a long time. We met at their offices, and within minutes, were seated at my first of many 3 hour Spanish lunches, not to mention the 3 hour Spanish dinners which never started before 10.30p.m., that being the Spanish custom.

The damage fascism did was to the spirit and character of the Spanish. Certainly not to the material side of life for, if you could afford it, there was no shortage of splendid restaurants offering high cuisine in comfortable surroundings. There was a feeling of a step back in time, the middle and upper classes had, on the whole, given support to the Loyalist regime (i.e., Franco), and the existence of servants, even of family retainers, seemed a throwback not to England in the Thirties but to an Edwardian era. But it made a pleasant life; just play it our way, don Alfonso, there is no reason you should not enjoy the same life style as hitherto. And life for the visitor was very, very cheap. Hotels were about half the price of provincial U.K. and food in or out of restaurants the same. Ignacio Iloduya, who accompanied me on the visits to foundries which investigation and research had thrown up as potential customers, always used a hire car, complete with driver, one Manuel. Always Manuel and we made visits within a radius of 50 – 60 miles of Bilbao, at a hire cost of £1 per day. In the evening, between 6 and 7 o'clock, I had my first experience of the "Paseo". This is peculiarly Spanish. The whole of a town's population seems to descend on the centre. The young men and girls in their best clothes sauntering slowly in separate groups, eyeing each other, not speaking and certainly not touching, the girls frequently with a chaperone. I was sitting in a bar, open to the street, drinking and observing. I paid a brief visit to the lavatory, perhaps an absence of two minutes, and to my astonishment, when I returned the street was empty. The paseo was over and everybody had gone home. It was as though a huge flock of starlings on the pavement had suddenly, silently flown off.

After a week I left Bilbao to motor South West to Valencia, where I had several appointments to keep and a lecture to deliver. If, in those days, there was a real Spain to be seen it was there in all its stark reality – empty roads, badly damaged showing little attempt at repair, only a handful of vehicles encountered in the 150miles to Burgos, an ancient town, also in bad repair. Barren hills, a few inhabited hovels off the road which, except for the brilliant sunlight, could have been in the West of Ireland during the 1850 potato famine. A wider, but still poorly surfaced road to Madrid, and again an absence of wheeled traffic. I turned onto something hardly more than a track 50 miles from Madrid towards Guadalajara. Twisting steep sided road, scene of much fighting, Cuenca, then through the hills to Teruel, in Winter said to be the coldest place in Spain. Walled and bitterly contested in 1937 in temperatures of −20°C. The British Battalion caught a packet there and an unknown soldier wrote:

Eyes of men running, falling, screaming,
Eyes of men shouting, sweating, bleeding,
The eyes of the fearful, those of the sad,
The eyes of exhaustion, and those of the mad.

A hard trek to Valencia, 450 miles of desolation and poverty all too visible. And yet – and yet a people full of dignity, you saw it in the faces. They had suffered so much over the centuries, but were not yet hammered into the ground. But Valencia seemed hardly touched, and was a typical Mediterranean town, wide boulevards, palm lined, many churches with strong Arab influence. When one observes today the modest contribution by the Islamic states to the arts, sciences and architecture it is hard to understand the Moorish/Arab 700 years of occupation of Spain during which their contribution to civilisation, particularly in the arts, and sciences was astonishing, compared with that of the Catholic Church. When they finally withdrew in 1492, after years of war, Spain was the loser and it was a very long time before tolerance, especially towards the Jews, and good government, exhibited at every level by the Moors, returned to Spain.

The business completed in Valencia, the long drive West began, North towards Madrid, then West to Toledo, a towering fortress and where one of the great stories of the Civil War was enacted. In July 1937 it was occupied by Franco's forces under Col. Moscado. Heavily attacked by the Republican militia, he retreated to the Alcazar, half fortress, half palace set on a hill commanding the city and the River Tagus. It was virtually impregnable and without it Toledo could not be completely taken. The Republican commander telephoned Moscado to say that his son, Luis, had been captured and would be shot unless the Alcazar surrendered. Luis was put on the phone and the father said "What is happening, my boy?" "Nothing, but they say they will shoot me if you do not surrender the Alcazar" said Luis. "If it be true" said his father "Commend your soul to God, shout Viva España! And die like a hero". Luis was shot, though not immediately. The Alcazar was relieved after two months. This story was put about by the Republicans as propaganda, but was authenticated later. When Franco's forces entered Toledo they slaughtered every Republican soldier in the city, and that is Civil War for you, in all its nastiness.

The centre of Spain is a vast area of brown aridity, few trees. Low hills North and South relieve the tedium of complete isolation in the absence of people and movement. Everything was so still, so silent. Many miles between the small, ancient towns of Talavera de la Reina, Merida and Badajoz on the Portuguese border, where I was to stay the night, 500 miles from Valencia. There were few villages and not many people about as I drove through. Already, although only mid-May, the torrid thrusting heat of North Africa could be felt, and the chirping of the male cicadas seemed never silent. I was beginning to understand how big Spain was, twice the area of the U.K. but with less than half the population.

There was one small, compact, interesting town, which appeared relatively prosperous, Merida. Old, very old, with evidence of Roman occupation, a temple and a forum. But it was something else which drew my attention. Firstly the heavy, musky perfume of the rose bushes which lined the main avenue, and the happy sight of many babies and children being accompanied on their walk by nannies, not just any old nannies, but looking like the product of the London Norland School of nannies which for a hundred years trained middle class girls as nannies for the aristocracy. It was another of those steps back through time to which I was becoming accustomed. Norland nannies are still trained in London but I am told that they are now so superior that they interview the prospective client, rather than the reverse. The first village I passed through, just over the border from France, had at its entrance and exit a pair of soldiers, armed of course. Then every village I passed through thereafter had the same. Wearing three cornered hats made of patent leather and in green uniforms, they were members of the Civil Guard, the most universally detested body in the whole of Spain since the Inquisition. In a population of eleven million they numbered 30,000 in 1936 and considerably more in 1952, as they were now a quasi military police force. They never served in the part of Spain from whence they came, and were not encouraged to speak to anyone in the village in which they were quartered. They had a deserved reputation for ruthlessness. "When one joins the Civil Guard", it was remarked, "one declares civil war". In a work force of four and a half millions, agricultural workers employed by the day, sometimes on a pay of one peseta a day, need watching. The Civil Guard was just the force to do it.

Badajoz, on the River Guardina, small, walls twenty feet high and a river bridge built by the Romans, the scene of the bloodiest battle of the Peninsular War. In April 1812 the French held the town with a force numerically superior to the British. On the 15th at 10p.m., the walls were stormed and by 6a.m. the next morning a breech was made and the British were in the town. Such savagery, over 5,000 of the attackers lay dead and as many wounded. Because the attack was resisted, what followed had been normal since the Middle Ages. The soldiers went mad on drink and hatred. Rape and murder went on for two days and then Wellington erected a gallows, and after a few hangings everything quietened down.

Wellington, not a man to show his emotions, is said to have wept at the butcher's bill.

Badajoz, a dramatic looking town with a decent hotel, and a paradore. The Government built these paradores to a high standard, frequently in castles as at Badajoz, and in 18th/19th century houses. The comfort and food was just about the best to be found in Spain.

Next morning I crossed, with no trouble, into quite another land, another fascist dictatorship quite different to that of Franco. Portugal (Dr.Salazar – proprietor) is green. If I were forced to describe a country by a single word that is the word I would use for Portugal. The climate is temperate, warmish wet Winters, quite hot and dry in Summer. Ideal for crops of all sorts, including wine, both red and white, with the reds of quite outstanding quality measured against the world's standards. So plenty of food, wine, fish of bountiful quantity and quality. Nobody starving, no cruel vindictive police covert or overt, as in Russia, and no war since 1800, the Peninsula War being fought almost entirely over the border in Spain. Why then did such a country need a dictator? There was little industry up until the late '40's and the agricultural way of life was the only way and it provided a mere subsistence for a large, landless peasantry. It was more like 18th century Ireland than 20th century Europe with a landed upper class that ruled the roost, the cock crowing on the top of the dung heap. What they had they were determined to hold and there was nothing odd about that in the 20th century A.D. I fancy it was the proximity of that part of Spain where the lot of the peasant was even worse, since the land was poor, the rain was scarce, the crops meagre and the daily pay at starvation levels, which acted as a contagion affecting the Portuguese day labourers across the border who started to become stroppy. Thus, Salazar, a Professor of economics at the University of Coimbra, was asked b y the Government to sort out the economics and commercial problems of the country in 1930. A sort of John Maynard Keynes, but with executive authority. It seems that he slid into the role of dictator almost by accident. But however it was in 1952, clearly he was the boss. There were no political parties with any power, law and order were administered from Lisbon and little or no nationalisation of Production, Distribution and Exchange, the famous Clause 4 of the U.K. Labour

Party. Business, manufacture, buying and selling were largely free of the dead hand of beaurocracy and people, by and large, were free to come and go as they wished, provided they obeyed the golden rule "Keep your trap shut, don't criticise the government and avoid the spreading of subversion, the nature of which we, the government, will be the judges."

A lovely drive, an easy 150 miles through undulating, empty country, few villages, and not a single town of consequence before crossing the River Tagus into the handsome, architecturally adventurous city of Lisbon. Meetings with my agent, Oliviera, the industrial section of Blandy Brothers, 19th century English growers and traders in Madeira wine on the island of Madeira since 1810, followed, and many meetings and visits to foundries of all descriptions around Lisbon but more so along the 200 miles of road leading to Porto in the North. For some reason the English here always added an "o", calling it Oporto. Nobody could tell me why. Quite a number of foundries were family affairs and it was the custom for the owner to have his handsome house adjacent to the works, behind walls. When the works were closed, a dog or dogs of alarming size and savagery were loose in the garden. It was not a place to visit after dark. People of Lisbon affected detestation for Porto, and said the only decent road there was the one back to Lisbon. Samuel Johnson, I recall, held the same view about Scotland and the road back to England.

As a visitor, as far as travelling, hotels, eating and general getting about was concerned you could have been in any Western town. The principal difference being, as in Spain, almost obscenely low prices reflecting low wages. A few miles West of Lisbon along the lovely Atlantic coast are the tiny resorts of Estoril and Cascais. There many exiled European Kings and Princes lived in idyllic surroundings In Estoril at the Palaccio Hotel which, complete with Casino, was a dead ringer for the Hotel de France in Monte Carlo, my stay of several days cost £3.50 per day for a suite of three rooms, half pension. Despite life being somewhat easier for the people, there was something downtrodden about the Portuguese. Greater poverty and suffering seemed to have given the Spaniards greater dignity.

Portugal was developing an industrial base, principally because Western Europe was hungry for consumer goods, and an educated middle class plus an obedient working class were ideally situated to exploit niches in a variety of markets. The Government was sympathetic to this as it would do much to improve the living standards overall. It did, of course, also develop dangers for, if you increased your urban industrial base, you increased also the social and political involvement of the work force, as the unions, though banned, covertly increased their strength. Inevitably, on the death of Salazar in 1970, there was a steady movement towards full democracy which was reached in 1974.

Lisbon and Porto could not be more different. The former is sophisticated, metropolitan and urbane in thinking, within the reins allowed by Salazar. Porto is rustic and devout, with overtones of an earlier century when the Church's puritanism ruled all family behaviour with an iron fist. In the streets the men outnumbered the women greatly and in the cafés and bars women, except of a certain profession, were rarely to be seen.

The entrance to the town with Lisbon behind you is dramatic. A long bridge spans the River Douro. Indeed, it spanned a deep gorge of 150 feet, the river flowing left to the port and to the right it came down from the steep slopes in the West. There are many claimants to being the most spectacular vineyards, the vine clad slopes of the Rhine and Mosel, and those steeper still in Switzerland, but these all fall short of the high drama of the Douro, almost uninhabited except for tiny clusters of dwellings among the steep terraced acres of vineyards down to the river. The Douro is never placid, in places surging through narrow gorges, it was often perilous for the special boats laden with the barrels of red wine mixed with 25% of grape brandy. Each vessel contains a pipe (110 gallons) on its way to the suburb of Porto Vila Nova da Gaia, in which the Anglo Scottish emigrès of the 18th century built the wine lodges and created the craft of blending the barreled wines from the valley of the Douro into Porto, the greatest of all the dessert wines. The red wines of the Douro are harsh, bitter, infamously alcoholic and, to northern palates, unpleasant. It took the genious of the British to make it drinkable. Looking over the bridge to the left your eye catches the names on the sides of the Lodges: Cockburn, Taylor, Graham, Croft, Sandeman, Dow, Warre and Delaforce. Many of these families, as I write, still live in Porto and for over three hundred years they sent the wine to the U.K., U.S.A., France, all the Anglo Saxon countries and many others.

It is curious, the affinity that fortified wines have for the British, for as they did in Portugal with port, so they did in France for cognac, on the island of Madeira for madeira wine, on the island of Sicily for marsala, and last, perhaps the most famous of all, sherry made in Jereth de la Frontera.

Now, sherry brings me to a strange story that started on the battlefield of Culloden in 1745, and ended with the death of a very old friend on the 22nd of October, 2002.

There was a family of Gordons, one of many Highland clans, which in the Jacobite Rebellion of 1745 elected to fight for the Young Pretender, Bonnie Prince Charlie. After the defeat at the Battle of Culloden in 1745, many of the Catholics of Scotland fled abroad to avoid capture, torture and almost certain execution in the nastiest possible way. Like most of the Highland clans they were Catholic recusants, refusing to recognise either the faux Protestant faith of Henry VIII or the Covenanters of Edinburgh. Finally in about 1780 this Gordon branch, or some of them, ended up in Jerez de la Frontera, planted vineyards, made fine sherries and prospered mightily. They intermarried with Domecq and Gonzales Biaz, the greatest of the sherry families. Finally a fair number of them, grandfathers, fathers, sons, daughters came back to the U.K. in 1905, and Louis' grandfather became the U.K. selling end of Domecq. By that time Spain had Gordons all over the sherry area, breeding prolifically as devout Catholics and, unlike Onan of Biblical notoriety, they spilt not their seed upon the ground. The Spanish Gordons are in Jerez today.

The family threw up a fair handful of eccentrics. One Alexander Gordon was publicly guillotined at Brest in 1769, supposedly as an English spy. Another, Juan José Gordon, went back to Woodhouse near Aberdeen as laird, as the Gordons had been for countless generations. At Woodhouse, he built a bull ring, imported Spanish bulls, and invited his Spanish friends to Woodhouse to practise the ancient craft of tauromachy.

I first met Luis George Anthony Maria Gordon, 20 years old and just married, in the George Hotel, Crawley, on a Saturday morning in 1954, a favourite watering hole of the Sussex jeunesse doré in those days. There were other Gordons alongside and Louis and I hit it off immediately. He had just had his 21st birthday at which the pipe of port (110 gallons) laid down by his father on the day of his birth was broached. We met frequently thereafter until a few months before his death. He played the largest possible part in putting Domecq on the U.K. sherry map, and added a new dimension to corporate entertainment when he chartered a Comet aeroplane, filled it with journalists, publicans and wine traders and flew them down to Jerez. Louis was no ordinary salesman. There, when they were drunk, he invited the guests to enter the ring and play with a bull or two.

In 1970 he bought a wine bar in Villiers Street alongside Charing Cross station. Coincidentally, it was called Gordon's Wine Bar, but no relation. That Gordon opened it in the 19th century and was the first in London. It is in a cellar, and was and is a dump, but Louis would never, ever, remove a single cobweb or clean away any dust. It serves all the fortified wines from the barrel, the food is very decent, and it is always full. As they say, le tout monde would come to Louis' Bar.

At the Memorial Service, many people could not get into the church, where they stood in the nave and the aisles. Louis died on 22nd October, 2002 AD, leaving six sons and Wendy, his wife. In 69 years he contributed greatly to the gaiety of life. Two weeks later Wendy threw a party at the wine bar and the cheerful boozers spilt out onto the pavement.

It would be perverse not to mention bull fighting, a corrida de toros, while in Spain for three weeks, my first visit. When in Bilbao I was taken by my friends to the small nearby town of Durango. There was a small bull ring, simple, even by provincial standards, and at that time of year before the season began it was the local tradition to view the bulls in the morning whom the young men would play with the cloak in the ring in the late afternoon. There was no sword play by a matador, or dart play (banderilleros), and the tips of the horns were bound in cloth. The bulls were no more than 18 months old, frisky but not too dangerous. The object was for the 16 – 18 year old young men to display machismo, and perhaps a little bravery, to the girls. The worst they usually suffered was a kicking or, if tossed, their friends were on hand to entice the bull away. This was a useful introduction and I learnt a lot from talking to people who thought of little else during much of the year.

In Valencia I saw my first fight. Valencia is provincial but not in bull fighting terms. It ranks with Madrid in sophisticated appreciation of the fighting bull, and a Valencianado will lavish praise and admiration on a matador who fights with skill and courage. Equally, he will hurl cushions or bottles at a poor performer who shows little skill and worse, cowardice. People who might fear the dentist's drill, paradoxically, show small sympathy to a man who just doesn't want to be killed by a bull.

The most important fights are on Sundays; and the first of six bulls goes into the ring at 5.30 sharp when the sun is still hot but well beyond the meridian, leaving the best seats in the shade. First there is a colourful march of the three matadors, each with his cuadrille (team) of banderilleros and picadors, to the sound of trumpets. They are preceded by two mounted men, alguacils, dressed in costumes of the time of Philip II who gallop across the ring, doff their caps to the president of the fight, and ask his permission to proceed. The matadors also halt and bow. The president then throws down the key which opens the red door behind which the first bull is waiting.

I was fortunate to have a seat in the barrera, two rows above where all three matadors stand in a narrow passage into which the bulls cannot squeeze. All three are together in case the one fighting is wounded or in danger and needs help. All is now ready, and the crowd silent. The red door is opened, and there is a pause of perhaps two seconds before a black shape hurls itself like a locomotive into the ring, jumps in the air with all four legs straight and blinks in the strong sun. That is a sight once seen and never to be forgotten. He then stopped, looked around, trotted the 30/40 yards across the sand towards the matador enticing him with the cape, rose coloured on the outside and yellow on the inside, dragging on the ground. The matador with the cape now extended into the air plays the bull, making him pass first one side of him and then the other, using his skill to get the bull always to follow the cape while getting perilously close the the horns. He does this many times in what is called a series of Veronicas. Veronicas after St. Veronica who, tradition has it, wiped the sweat from the face of Christ on his way to crucifixion. In Spain the symbolism of religion is never far from the bull ring. All this is to tire the bull, but he does not know yet that defeat is not far away.

The matador retreats behind his barrier and the picador trots up. Horses, for many years, have been protected against disembowelment by a heavy quilted material. The bull sees the horse and charges. The picador leans down and plunges his lance deep into the shoulder muscles, and holds it there while the bull tries, and sometimes succeeds, in lifting the horse off its feet. The picking may be done twice more by two other picadors, the operation being to weaken the bull. The ring is now cleared for the placing of the 3 feet darts (banderillas) into the bull. He is brought to the fight by the banderillero calling to him. As he charges, the banderillero runs towards him, leans over between the horns, plunges the darts in, and turns away in the air hoping to miss the horns. At that moment he is in great danger. He may do this again with two more pairs of darts. The bull is now tiring but very dangerous at close quarters. Now begins the third act in this tragedy, the execution.

The matador enters the ring, turns and bows to the president. With the muleta, a piece of heavy red cloth attached along its width to a wooden stave, in one hand, and the killing sword in the other, he calls out to his protagonist, and as he charges the muleta, now held across the matador's body, is moved away, leading the bull away from the man's stomach. In a series of balletic moves the bull charges the muleta, first on one side, and then the other, with the man twisting in a small tight circle – if he is very brave. For the bull now is as dangerous as a wounded tiger. With the bull now totally bemused, the matador with his sword outstretched horizontally, now calls to the bull again, then goes in over the horns to find the one place, only two inches in diameter, into which to plunge the sword deep into the heart. If he misses, as he often does first time, the sword buckles against bone, so he must call for another sword. When the target is found the sword goes in deep and the brave bull slowly collapses and rolls over. Five more bulls follow to receive the same fate.

I never liked the use of the darts, but unless the bull is weakened the matador would be killed just about every time. As for the bull, he will have had four, maybe five, years living like a sultan, pampered in great comfort and built up to his fighting weight of nearly half a ton. Then, instead of being taken to an abattoir and ignominiously slaughtered, he dies fighting, and sometimes kills his opponent.

Some matadors have as many as 90 fights a year. They must live in a state of constant terror. What sort of man will do this? Certainly not one to hug and kiss his fellow matadors, and rub each other's heads like monkeys, as do our brave footballers. The bull fight is neither a sport nor a game; it is a tragic contest played out between a brave bull and a brave man. It is very Spanish and could never take root in an Anglo Saxon land. It is to do with the different way in which death is regarded.

Many years ago, an American resident in Spain, told me a story that uniquely describes how different Spain is in the matter of the bull and bull fighting. A Papal edict of 20th November 1567 was issued in which bull fighting was allowed provided a bull was not permitted to live and fight again. This was because many men had been killed by bulls allowed to fight more than once – they are quick learners. But small provincial towns, desperately poor, could not afford to replace bulls as they were too costly. It became the practice to create a fighting arena by blocking up all exits and entrances to a town square and use it for a practice place for as-piring but poor matadors. This was a savage and primitive sport and in one such town a bull, over a period of years, killed 16 men and boys and wounded over 60. This bull was killed in a very odd way. One of those killed was a gypsy boy of fourteen. Afterwards the boy's brother and sister followed the bull around hoping, perhaps, to assassinate him. They fol-lowed him for two years and then the town decided to send him for slaughter and buy another. The two gypsies were at the abattoir and asked if they could carry out the killing. Permission granted, the boy started by gouging out the bull's eyes and spitting carefully into the sockets. He then severed the spinal marrow between the neck vertebrae, with some diffi-culty and cut off the bull's testicles. Then he and his sister lit a fire in the street, roasted and ate them. It is said that revenge is a dish best eaten cold, but it seems the gypsy prefers it hot.

Over the next 30 years many visits were made to the Iberian Peninsula but it was not until the death of Salazar in 1972, and Franco in 1975, that great sea changes were enacted. It was as though the unused, unperceived talents of two great peoples, unnaturally imprisoned, were suddenly freed, almost like the Berlin Wall coming down in November 1989. The lid was off the pressure cooker and within a couple of years the standard of living shot up. There was little or no industrial strife though more in Portugal than Spain, and within a few months they were pulled joyfully from the

19th century into the 20th. It was amusing to see the girls smoking like chimneys in the street and riding astride on their boyfriend's motorbikes, instead of demurely sidesaddle. And they mingled and talked together during the paseo every evening. Franco must have turned in his grave. Democracy in its truest sense had arrived and the hated Civil Guard was brought swiftly under control.

How much do the countless millions holidaying in Spain and Portugal now know of the sufferings of those two peoples which was necessary before the freedom of their holidays became possible?

FRANCE

When someone widely considered to be the greatest Frenchman of the 20th century, even if better known for his bad breath, addiction to Gauloise cigarettes and sticking two fingers up to Harold MacMillan in 1963 who was pleading with him to let us join the Common Market, says that, we MUST take notice.

Twentysix miles away, yet to some people France might just as well be next to Ulan Bator. Yet, and yet, the ink on the Treaty of Amiens in 1802 which bisected the Napoleanic War was barely dry when the dandies, bucks and hoi polloi of London were on the quayside at Dover waiting for the first ferry to Calais for nine years, and then on to Paris. The exquisite fleshpots, naughty clothes, etcetera (especially the etceteras) were calling. The English have long pretended to hate the French and the French to despise the English. There is nothing wrong with that, such opinions, false or true, have always been good for books or newspapers; and France never ceases to raise an enticing finger. Mt first visit was in 1948 and last in 2003 and, except for a period of two years (of which more later) in the 1960's, have been there several times, sometimes many times, each year.

They called our 19th century soldiers "Rosbifs" and "Goddams". We called them "Filthy French Frogs". Now, I understand, they call out football yobs, descendents of those brave soldiers of Wellington "The Fuck-offs". Terms of endearment really, like the Australians calling us "Pommy Bastards". Dickens always ranted and raved about France but kept going there. "It is an unsettled question with me", he wrote "whether I shall leave Calais something handsome in my will or whether I shall leave it my malediction. I hate it so much yet I am always glad to see it."

My wife and I first went there in July 1948for the 14th July celebrations, le Quatorze Juillet, always a great time to be in Paris. We were all but broke but the boat from Newhaven to Dieppe, then train to Gare St. Lazaire, followed by seven days pure elixir of delight, cost less than twenty quid door to door. Our room in Rue de St.André des Arts in the Buci Market, St. Germain-des-Prés, was a dirty dump but was only a hefty stone's throw from Brasserie Lipp, Café de Flore and les Deux Magots, where the likes of Colette, Juliette Greco and Jean Paul Sartre and the rest of the pretentious existentialists held court daily. Hovel it may have been, corridors lit by 20 watt bulbs which went out after ten seconds, and drains of a familiar odour. But what do you expect for six shillings and eight pence per night, the Ritz? Why should I remember a price of six shillings and eight pence? Unforgettable because, after fifty years, it was still the price a solicitor would charge you for sending a letter to a stroppy neighbour. So there you have it, the love-hate relationship between the English and the French, as strong today as in Charles Dickens time and probably unchanged since the battle of Hastings.

It was the Spring of 1953 when I first drove in France, and that was to Spain. From then onwards, at intervals of rarely more than two weeks between trips, I departed by car on the Dover or Folkestone ferryboat to points North, East, South or South West. Going North or East the first part of the journey

was to Aachen, and from there to Dusseldorf, Hanover, Hamburg or Cologne, Frankfort, Stuttgart or Munich, to Vienna and points further East or South. Those routes were positive 'milk runs' until 1969, after which my journeys tended to be entirely within the Common Market countries with an occasional foray into Scandinavia. The one absolute common factor was Calais. Calais was where I started from and it was to Calais I came back, unless I was very late when it had to be Dunkirk or Ostend. For a few years it was a great luxury to be able to fly with a car from Lydd in Kent to Le Touquet, Calais or Ostend. It was a journey of 20 – 30 minutes with a landing on grass. In those years also you could fly from the centre of Brussels to the centre of Paris, and from Paris to Bordeaux by helicopter. Not any more – who was it that said things always get worse? That old curmudgeon Kingsley Amis, I think.

You can get used to anything in time, even the cobbled roads all the way to Paris, Lille, Brussels, in fact, just about everywhere in Northern

France. Pavé roads were steeply cambered, allowing the rain to drain off. So in a right hand drive you drove permanently tilted to the right at an angle of 20° which was most uncomfortable.

In the early days of the long drives, apart from timing how long a Polomint could be retained in the mouth before breaking up, it was amusing to dwell on those things in which we differed from the Continentals, and how they may have influenced the way we thought and acted. The wedding ring, from Moscow to Lisbon, is worn on the right hand. Salt is always contained in a pot similar to pepper, a pot with many holes instead of a single hole. If you are lucky enough to get eggs and bacon for breakfast, the eggs are always broken over the bacon so that they fry together. They get married with the bridegroom wearing a dinner jacket, or tuxedo, as the Americans call it. They have their elections on Sundays, not as we do on Thursdays. And, most menacing of all, at level crossings the barrier closes vertically, not horizontally, as did ours but not any more. There is still a frisson of fear

when driving under that huge pole stuck in the air. With such basic differences between us can we ever form an homogenous people?

Kilometres never troubled me, neither did kilograms. Changing to miles is an easy piece of mental arithmetic, multiply by five then divide by eight. Such harmless devices did much to reduce journey times. But how long before our masters rob us of our miles, and how long will a cricket pitch be when it is no longer twentytwo yards? The centres of industry in France are diverse, not conveniently grouped together as in Birmingham, the Black Country, Manchester, Sheffield or Glasgow. The industrial revolution came much later to France, railways and good roads also. That is why the car was the best and most economical way to travel on business. Industrial plants were mostly a long way from airports, and trains a long way from plants as well. It took the most inclement weather to delay an experienced driver. Airports may be closed, but it took deep snow to halt a car. In the 1950's it was surprising how little countries knew about each other. An island race grows up thinking itself superior to all others, few of whom he has ever met. In the case of the British, confident in the superiority of its industrial skills and quality of its manufactured goods over all others, it cam as a surprise to find that the French had equal skills, and goods of excellent quality. By the 1970's it was very disturbing that in the matter of skills and quality they more often than not exceeded us.

Looking beyond Luddite trades unions, and a succession of Labour governments, dirigiste, and wedded to nationisation, there was a malaise, a growth in a dependency culture, which may have had its origins in the state education system. The Continentals were better educated, and this, when the money became available, improved their industry, which didn't have the unproductive weight of nationisation on its back, because management and workers were better trained. This increased production, lowered costs, created exports, built motor roads, a marvellous railway network and a very good health care service for everybody.

It has never ceased to puzzle and also anger me why, at the extremes of British society, both the upper and two lower classes have such contempt and resistance to education and to the law. In other matters also they show disturbing similarities. Today I believe the gap between the Continentals and us continues to widen. Not that I want to live away from England. I am simply glad that at frequent intervals I am able to travel in France, Germany, Italy, Switzerland and the other countries,

if only for the weather.

On first testing the water, as it were, my impression of the Pas de Calais from, say, Dunkirk down to Boulogne, was of dowdiness, shabbiness, but not poverty. The houses had not had a lick of paint since 1914. What irony it was to see, at regular intervals along the main roads, the advertisement:

VALENTINE LES BELLES PENTURES

Did Valentine S.A. have any customers for its paints? Another amusing advert. was:

PERRIER L'EAU QUI CHANTE ET QUI DANSE

There were few people in the restaurants that suited my pocket drinking expensive bottled water. Tap water mixed with cheap red wine was more likely.

Car ownership was at a low level in the 1950's and roads deserted until, that is, 12 o'clock when the daily dash home for lunch began. There were few works canteens and no self-respecting French worker would lunch on sandwiches. Breakfast from choice was a bowl of milky coffee into which bread was dunked, usually stale from the previous day, at 06.30. By mid-day they were tetchy if not downright bad tempered, brought on by hunger, and so they raced home by bicycle, moped or car for a proper meal. It took two hours but then they worked late to put in the full eight or nine hours, plus, of course, Saturday morning. It was pleasing all over Europe to be able to work on Saturday mornings up to about 1970. Saturday work had been abandoned in the U.K. years earlier, except as overtime, which the workers wanted even if the unions didn't.

There were relatively few cars, as prices were high and wages low. That is why, until the late 1960's when the French became rich, the two cars mostly to be seen were the Citröen van, always grey with corrugated metal sides and small windows and the other was the Citröen Deux Chevaux. They were cheaper, easy to park (two men could lift up the back and lift it into the gutter, or most likely onto the pavement. Farmers used them, mostly to take produce to market. Both were made at enormous car plants in the Paris area. At that time the standard of living was somewhat lower than in the U.K. but as far as food was concerned corners were not cut. Hotels were short on comforts, such as soap supply, very thin towels, and a complete absence of bathrooms in the provinces. The bidet, of course, was never missing from the bedroom as, to the French, it was necessary for personal hygiene, and, to the English, a source of much amusement. In Americans it aroused either puzzlement or disgust.

But in the matter of food, even in the meanest village in Eastern France, where poverty was occasionally observed, a poor meal a l'anglais would be rare. No powdered soup, no vegetables boiled for hours, no overcooked meat. There would be one knife, one fork, one spoon and a paper tablecloth on which the waiter wrote the bill.

Occasionally, in a large works such as Peugeot, one might be invited to take lunch in the canteen. The same kitchen prepared the same food for all, though management had its own seating area. And the quality was that of a good restaurant that valued its reputation. Wine was unstinted, though I could have been happier with less generous hospitality.

If I could offer a piece of advice, and I am not sure I should, for advice givers are rarely welcome, it is when in France try to avoid driving near the time of 2 o'clock when those who have lunched in a restaurant emerge, weaving a little before entering the car to drive unsteadily to their place of work. They can be dangerous and are best given a wide berth.

Lille was a memorable industrial town and a stranger could have imagined himself in an Eastern European town with its fumes and industrial squalor. They certainly were not buying Valentine's paints either. But again they prospered through hard work and the place, as it said in the Michelin Guide was "worth a detour".

Lyon now, that is a town of beauty and distinction with a surprising amount of industry, built on the back of its silk business. It was also full of great restaurants, many bearing a woman's name, Mère Brazier, Mère Guy, La Mère Vitet, Bistro de la Mère. I had visions of mothers, despairing of ever turning their sons into good chefs, failing, and going into the restaurant business themselves.

A probably mythical tale about Lyon is that it drinks more Beaujolais wine than is ever grown. This probably tells one more about Beaujolais than Lyon, for this pleasant, ordinary red wine through clever advertising and such things as Beaujolais Nouveau has become the best and sometimes the only French wine known to much of the world. Thus the fraudsters moved in, bought a lot of Beaujolais labels, slapped them on bottles full of cheap red wine and increased the sale tenfold. For such is the gullibility of people in the presence of clever advertising. Beaujolais is grown less than 50 miles from Lyon, so the Lyonnais, at least, should know better.

Once in late February 1960, passing through Montélimar at about 11am, thinking about lunch and in no hurry I remembered that in Vienne, an old Roman town of no particular distinction, there was a restaurant called La Pyramide regarded by many French as the greatest in the world. The patron was Monsieur Fernand Point, and stories I had read about him were both amusing and disturbing. He was inclined to be choosy and impressed neither by wealth or reputation. For example, there was the French Minister who appeared on the doorstep with a small entourage and requested a table. Point politely refused him, as a reservation had not been made. Then the American millionaire, much in the news, and his wife who *had* a booking arrived, were led to a table and said they did not have much time so could they be served quickly. Point told him, politely, that if he wanted "fast food" he was in the wrong restaurant, and should go to the Routier (truck drivers' café) a few miles up the road. I doubt if Point would have had much time for today's "A" list celebrities or TV celebrity cooks. What he did have time for were polite, well-mannered people who would respect his restaurant, his cooking and his staff.

Vienne is a few miles South of Lyon and I was there at about mid-day, a perfect time for lunch. La Pyramide was easy to find and, a little nervous, I walked in and was confronted by Point himself. A huge man, well over six feet in height and probably twenty stone in weight, he eyed me quizzically. I apologised for not having made a reservation, but was almost in Vienne before remembering it was the home of his restaurant, and could I possibly have a table? He looked at me again, probably guessed I was English from my accent and said "Certainly, Monsieur, it is February and a Monday, a good time to take pot luck. (Pot luck? At La Pyramide?) I was in. I won't dwell too much on the food. Haut cuisine does not excite me, but good food that is well presented gives great delight. Fernand Point was a master of his trade, and everything done by him and his staff was beyond reproach. He sat me down at a good table and with a glass of champagne in one hand he gave me one with the other. "I drink a couple of glasses in the morning, perhaps three over lunch but only a couple in the evening". He failed to say that it was a daily practice.

After about thirty minutes and another glass, the first hors d'oevres arrived, a cold paté en croute, followed in a few minutes by a fois gras trufflé, then a hot pheasant paté, and another and another and another. There was no menu, but a different one every day the restaurant was open during the year. There were no prices either. The hors d'oevres were followed by a truites au bleu accompanied by a white burgundy, a Chevalier Montrachet. Then there were slices from a leg of lamb, beautifully pink and accompanied by a red burgundy, La Täche, local cheese, a patisserie, coffee and a cognac or two. This by the standards of La Pyramide was grand but not formidable. It was, after all, February, and a Monday. It was nearing 4 o'clock and I was in a quandary, not short of money but not absolutely sure. Anyway, M. Point brought me the bill. When I saw it I was astounded, sure he had grossly undercharged me. True it was about three times bigger than I had ever paid in my life. "M. Point" I said "surely you have missed something out?" "Do you question my arithmetic, Monsieur?" he said. But he knew that I knew. We shook hands as I left and he said "Perhaps you will come again. February on a Monday is always a good time to try pot luck". He was quite old then but lived to be over 80, still drinking champagne.

There was a decent hotel nearby and I told the owner that I had just had lunch at La Pyramide. "So, you won't be needing dinner then". He was right. I went to bed and slept through until 6 o'clock next morning.

Almost exactly a year later, along with my American boss Herbert von Wolff and Réné, an engineer working for our French agent, I was driving from Belfort in Eastern France to Pont à Mousson near Metz. For two days we had been in the foundry of Peugeot Motors. It was a fine day with little traffic in no particular hurry and after perhaps 30 minutes driving, and passing through the village of Lure, something white flashed across our front from the right, and I hit it, a white Citroen D.S. more or less in the driver's door. In a second my car was on its side in a ditch to which I'd swerved. There was a deathly silence and I remember reaching up to switch off the ignition, and laughing a little, because I was still alive, I suppose. Then there were footsteps and hushed voices. We climbed out on the passenger side as my side was against the ground. At the time we had no idea about the other car and its driver though later we were informed he had broken his back and had other injuries. Both cars were write-offs. My boss had a broken wrist, Réné a cracked rib. The Citroen driver, according to the police, had come out of his house drive, across my line to drive to the right. His name was Maurice Moltoni, a local man and something of a jujitsu fighter. We were taken to the local hospital, run by nuns, who tried to fill us with suppositories, the French cure for everything, but left the next day. This affair between insurance companies and the lawyers took over two years to settle, going from one French court to another. During the next twelve months I drove through Lure three times. Each time a policeman on point duty recognised me as he was present at the accident, and greeted me with some warmth. Moltoni, he said, was a wife beater, a mother beater and was generally disliked in Lure. I was regarded as a public benefactor. Strangely, I tried several times to identify the exact place of the accident but failed. The memory plays tricks.

The next year was successful, and eventful, happily not in the Lure accident sense. Six times between March and November I motored South through Paris, Auxere, Dijon and Chalon-sur-Sâoneto Lyon. There were no motor roads then, just the long straight Routes 6 and 7, exciting, beautiful and dangerous with small sleepy villages and woodlands through to the vineyards of Burgundy. For those who may have read the trivial 1930's novels of Dornford Yates this road will be remembered. They were full of the gay (in the old sense of the word) and rich, the jeunesse d'oré of London society with names like Boy, Piers, Daphne and Ariadne. The men were tall and blonde, and so were the girls. Tearing down to the French Reviera in the open Rolls, no dark squat people ever got a place in a Dornford Yates novel.

In early March 1962, I left Milan at about mid-day to go home. The Simplon Pass to Switzerland was still closed with snow, but the regular car train service took me through the mountain tunnel, and fine weather, and good time was made from Brig in the Valais to Lausanne and the frontier crossing at Pontarlier into France in the direction of Besançon. Through the latter, I stopped at an auberge in a small village for food and a bed as it was now dark and I had had enough of driving, and went early to bed. Next morning the owner came down obligingly to let me out for I was leaving at 5am. It was still dark and his desk was dimly lit as I paid and left. The dawn was near to breaking and I could now see the beauty of this Département of the Dauphiné. There was rime on the empty road, frost on the undulating fields, and on the banks of the many streams and it felt good to be going home. But Nemesis was after me. It was light when I reached Chalon-en-Champagne and I stopped to fill up, thinking also I might get coffee and a croissant somewhere. Looking in my pocket for money to pay for the petrol I pulled out what should have been a 1,000 franc note, but magically it had turned into a 100 franc note, the larger one having been left on the desk at the auberge. I was now faced with the daunting task of explaining to a French garagist why I couldn't pay him. I offered him my watch in payment, and was quite beyond words when he accepted it. He couldn't have known much about watches. It kept bad time. I had bought it several years before in a dockside bar in Copenhagen from a broke Danish sailor. So far so good. A strange spin-off of that barter deal was that I never wore a watch again up to the present day.

Calais was only about six hours away – I thought. Outside Arras I had a blow out and lost half an hour changing the wheel. Outside a tiny place called Aire, some miles short of St.Omer I had another puncture. Now I was getting very deep into the merde. The Winter Ferry Time Table was in operation and the last boat left at about 3.30. I shut my eyes to rest a bit but woke to a tapping on the window. It was a polite man who asked if I was in trouble so I told him my tale. "Alright" he said "I'll drive you to a repair garage about 10km back where you can get a tyre repaired". I'm in luck again I thought. Now, in a country notorious for its fast drivers, what sort of luck do you need to have chosen the slowest driver in France when what you require was a Stirling Moss? By the time that tyre was re-paired, which took the last of my money, and fitted on the car I had lost a good one and a half hours, and certainly the ferry. He was such a nice man it would have been churlish to have displayed impatience. Later I wished I had begged a loan from him. He would have obliged, I am sure.

It was cold. I'd neither eaten nor drunk since 8 o'clock the previous evening. I had no money and the AA office was shut where I might have got a few francs. All I could do was walk about and wait in my car until six o'clock next day. It was VERY cold.

What did that old bugger Macmillan say? "Export is fun"?

I was even more pleased than usual to get home.

THE USA (PART I) AVETE

YOU SHOULD TRY EVERYTHING ONCE,

EXCEPT INCEST AND FOLK DANCING

That epitomizes your average citizen of America. If you fail in one thing, try another, and if you fail in something you know is a sure fire winner, go back to the drawing board and stay there until you've got it. Nowhere in the world is there to be found such determination to succeed, or such stigma attached to failure, or lack of bottle.

In 1958 I went to the U.S.A. for the first time. They seemed an odd people. "Two nations divided by a common language" said Oscar Wilde on his first visit; and I felt a stranger, more so than in any European country. Even in Yugoslavia, without a word of Serbo-Croat, I felt more at home. At first I put it down to being too much a European and, at 38, too old to fall into the Anglo American mode of communication which the young of today find easy.

A few months earlier I had changed jobs, leaving the employ of Lord Trefgarne to join an American corporation based in Cleveland, Ohio. They had a greater international exposure and were prepared to give me more freedom of action, and a damn sight more money. All one had to do was to succeed and back up talk with action. That is the good old American way. My appointment was Field Manager, Europe, and my job to appoint agents in every European country, to instruct them, and to assist in the negotiation of contracts with the larger companies such as Ford, Mercedes Benz, Volkswagen, Fiat and others in many industries. But it was a strange place. Even the smells were different. And the silence; to go into a bar out of brilliant sunlight was to stumble into a Stygian blackness which, for a few seconds, left you absolutely blind. As sight returned you might see in the inadequate lighting several bodies sitting on stools, crouched over the bar, not talking, not looking, just staring ahead. There was none of the noise, the banter or, to use a good German expression, to which there is no absolute English equivalent, "Gemütlichkeit", a sort of good natured homeliness. After a mistake or two I found it best not to make eye contact, considered at best provocation "What are you looking at?", or, at worst, damned dangerous, especially if the bloke was drunk, and felt threatened on hearing a foreign voice as English – English was to an American in 1958. It is hard to understand the isolationism so common in the U.S.A. Not just from other countries but from other parts of the U.S.A. Generalisations are not always wise, but speaking to somebody in, say, Iowa in the mid West, it was not unusual to hear him speak with near hatred of New York Yankees, Southern rednecks, and San Francisco faggots (homosexuals).

Once you were away from large city conurbations you observed the sameness between living areas. They couldn't be called villages. They had a very wide main street (downtown) with roads off at right angles to the main street. There were no pubs but maybe a bar. There was a sign outside a shop reading "Mufflers". It was some days before I was curious enough to ask what a muffler might be and the answer was an exhaust pipe for a car, and muffler signs were everywhere. Already the age of specialisation in car spares had thrown up the items mufflers and tyres which were bought from a place which sold nothing else. It was many years before such specialisation reached the U.K. and Europe. This was followed by sellers of break linings, dynamos and electric motors. All of which in the U.K. would have been bought from the garage that maintained one's car. It was such specialisation that helped make American cars so much cheaper than those made in the U.K.

In these dwelling places there was more silence. Though it might have been a community of a thousand, there were no children running about shouting and being naughty and not many adults either. Another eye catching place was the pawn shop and, cheek by jowl, a gun shop. I wondered, was there a connecting door? How many guns were pawned and reclaimed and were they, in fact, run as a single business? One should remember the influence of protestant puritanism, which was powerful all over. And there were still some States, mostly in the South, where alcohol, even 26 years after the repeal of the Prohibition Act by Roosevelt, was not sold. In the absence of bars and other drinking places the centre, the centre where the people gathered and organised their social lives was the Church, or, rather, Churches, for even in a small place there were more churches, chapels and tin tabernacles belonging to more denominations of the Christian faith than you could count on your fingers and toes, and one bar. Unlike Ireland where in a town there would be one church and twenty pubs.

Yet, as one visit to the U.S.A. followed another, for many years, the last being in the year 2000, I became less critical, more admiring and appreciative of what, at first encounter, appeared to be idiocyncracies but were the normal development of a people, mostly of European origin, who did things in their own way. They were cut off by time and distance from their origins but determined to make a better job of living their lives. It would be a harsh and prejudiced critic who would say they had failed. Or that in the fields of science, engineering, arts, innovation and especially democratic government they were not our equals, or, dare I say it, our superiors.

American food is criticised, especially by the French and others, on many counts such as blandness, lack of savour, and overzealous on the question of hygiene. The latter is certainly true, the old English saying "You've got to eat a peck of dirt before you die" is not known in America. One side issue of that is they are so protected from the modest degree of tummy upset encountered, though only occasionally in, say, Europe, that they have no immunity from such experiences. In my own case, having been exposed to the hazards of eating in India, the Balkans and the Middle East for over 50 years, I can count on one hand the times I fell victim to guts trouble. By contrast, my American boss who visited me twice a year, happily never for more than a few days, always got the shits after his first meal in France. In one restaurant of such Michelin splendour that to mention, just casually, that you had lunched there accorded you great respect, he was also given a bad dose of the runs.

Anyway for the next three weeks the work practices, and general way of getting things designed, built and sold were disclosed to me. It was an education and one you could only get in the U.S.A. I once saw above a desk in a U.K. plant, the following:

ANATOMY OF A DESIGN:

1) Enthusiasm

2) Panic

3) Search for the guilty

4) Punishment of the innocent

5) Congratulations all round to non-participants

It was a joke, perhaps ironical, perhaps not, but in the U.K. it was more likely to be true than in the U.S.A. In the 1960's there was a book written by Anthony Sampson called "The Anatomy of Power" and he wrote it about the British Civil Service. It included a phrase never to be forgotten: "The Civil Service is more concerned with the concealment of truth than the avoidance of error". Unhappily this attitude was positively endemic throughout the higher echelons of British industry, worst, of course, within the nationalised and public sectors. The aim of senior managers was to become error proof. It was as though James Watt, George Stevenson and Isambard Kingdom Brunel had never lived.

It was refreshing within the U.S.A. not to encounter the many failings of British industry that, over several generations, had dropped us in the league tables of entrepreneurial nations. If risk taking struck terror among managers in the U.K. it seemed to act like an aphrodisiac in the U.S.A. Part of the reason is that, whereas in the U.K. the heads of large industrial companies tend to be accountants, in the U.S.A and also in Germany, France and Italy, our main competitors, they are more usually engineers. That is the prime reason why our investment in capital plant has always been too small, because the accountants want the cost to be written off in two to three years, against the three to five years common in other countries. In short, our companies are headed by bureaucrats. The relationship between workers at all levels I found to be casual and lacking in protocol with little presumption on rank. Discussion where the interests of the company was concerned was open and encouraged. As a general statement, and based entirely on my experience, I think that the work place was more pleasant than in the U.K. If I had a criticism, it was that Americans took the working in teams to extremes and were not comfortable in being alone. In fact, they were never satisfied with their own company.

Perhaps I am just as bad for, on the whole, I prefer my own company, except for that of a small group of friends.

Fellow engineers of my company and myself spent the next three weeks visiting customer's plants and discussing new projects with potential clients. How different from what passed for customer liaison in the U.K. When a visit was to correct a machine malfunction, the first act of the American would be to put on overalls, or coveralls as they call them. The boss would treat us pleasantly or angrily, depending on the extent that the trouble with the machine was causing to production, and tell us to get on with it, providing any backup that may be required in the way of labour, tools or other equipment. The job would then be started and continue until the machine was ready for production again, however long it took, one h our or twenty hours. A machine not working could be costing $500 an hour of lost production.

By contrast in the U.K., and remember I am writing of the 50's and 60's which were the bad old days, a fitter might arrive at a plant in his best suit and suede shoes, as though he was going to a Saturday night dance, and leave his filthy overalls lying across the bench in his workshop. He might not even meet the boss, just being told to get on with it. Such attitudes frequently meant that several visits, sometimes by different personnel, were necessary before the non-appearing boss was satisfied. Also, in the U.S.A., the salesman responsible for the sale would either attend the job with the fitter or engineer or, in most cases, have the practical training, both electrical and mechanical, to do the work himself. During my visit this was always the case.

On the question of selling, one of the most honoured words in American business vocabulary is "Salesman". How often in the U.K. have you heard it said, spat out with contempt even, "Oh! Him! He's just a sales rep."? In America, when a firm is in trouble, short of work, the country or state in a gathering condition of recession, who are the last people to be fired? The sales force. When the same conditions exist in the U.K. who are the first people to be fired? You've guessed it.

Once in Belgrade I was talking to an Austrian in the Grand Hotel Moscow, where we were both staying. He had spent the last month driving all over the six provinces of Jugoslavia, not easy travelling in 1957, seeking business for his company in Graz which was desperately short of work with 200 jobs on the line. It had been hard and stressful, both mentally and physically, but he seemed to have obtained sufficient orders to keep his company busy for the next six months. We drank his health, and his firm's, and Tito's for good measure far into the night. A salesman can never be a jobsworth.

Looked at as a sales and marketing prospect, the size of the U.S.A. can appear alarming. The population was about 230 millions but spread over nine and a half million square miles, i.e., ninetyfive times the area of the U.K. Huge States such as Arizona, Arkansas, Ohio and Idaho were sparsely populated. The U.S.A. is a country of small towns, mostly smaller than in the U.K., with considerable distance between them and, of course, foundries and engineering works. A strange spin-off from this, bearing in mind that the Americans are considered rootless, and constantly on the move, is the reluctance to change jobs. The next plant that could employ your skills may be several hundred miles away. Such a condition can keep a man loyal to his company and his town. That said, I was touched by the courtesy and warm welcome extended to me, a visitor, in such places as North Platte, Nebraska, or Anoka, Minnesota.

One thing you could be certain of, never seeing in the U.S.A. a notice often seen in England: "Salesmen only seen between 10 a.m. and 3 p.m. on Mondays, and only then by appointment"

Very similar to those other good old English put downs, visible in greengrocers:

"Don't touch me 'til I'm yours.", and,

"Please do not ask for credit, as a refusal may offend."

In the U.S.A. the attitude towards the motor car was not comparable with that in the U.K. At home, the car was a luxury, a bench mark of a position in the pecking order: at one end the Rolls Royce, at the other a three wheeler. In the 1950's to have one put you in a substantial minority of about three million owners. There were another seven millions who yearned for one and would get it one way or another in the next 20 years, and many, many more in the next 30 years.

It was something to preen yourself on possessing, especially in the presence of a carless neigbour, and to suffer gloom and maniacal rage should it be scratched. But how to get one? The gathering of competitive brochures to study the contents became a job to outweigh the real job which supported your family, the perfunctory examination of available cash and credit, the outrageous acts of self deception as you snatched at the pros which proved you needed a car and the contemptuous dismissal of the cons which suggested you could not afford one. You would probably be frightened to drive it, worse your wife would learn to drive and, worst of all, one of your under age sons without any experience would take it out, drive it with the panache of the young and cocky, and crash it. Bloody hell, what was a man to do? I hope I may be forgiven the quotation of Christ in the Gospel of St. Luke, where he addresses a gathering of Pharisees, "You lawyers place such burdens on mankind too heavy to be borne.". Substitute "car ownership" for "you lawyers" and you have it in a nutshell.

However, aid to the non car owner was at hand. No need to worry how to pay for a car, you were going to get one for nothing, or practically nothing. Just as the use of credit card gives you the ephemeral feeling that without money actually changing hands the goods shoved into your paw by a shop assistant was a gift, and car ownership entered the same category.

It was in the period 1973/1976. Wilson had just kicked out Heath and not for the first time since 1945 the Labour Government was making another pig's ear of the country. Inflation was up, wage demands were through the roof, and the unions were leading us not a merry dance, rather a dance of industrial death. But help was at hand. Jack Jones, leader of the Transport and General Workers Union, had a spiffing wheeze. "Let's put an end", said Jack "to the workers getting a rise of £5 per week while the directors get £500. Let the maximum be £10 a week. Jaws dropped all round in the smoke filled room wherein union leaders fraternised with craven hearted ministers desperate for something to get them off the hook. So that was that, no pay rises above a tenner a week. And what did the bosses do? The accountants, traditionally on nobody's side but their own, said "Give all the middle managers a works car in lieu of a rise". Now wasn't that a splendid idea of Jack's? And it wasn't only middle managers who got their car on the firm. Just about anybody that could loosely be described as a key worker got a car. The car companies were ecstatic and production boomed. At least when the union leaders allowed their members to turn up. And that was how the problem of scraping and scrimping to buy a car was removed from tens of thousands of employees. Simple.

America had always had industrial troubles but not industrial anarchy and subversion of the body politic, which was our lot for a generation. The union had never been powerful, even in the car plants of Detroit, and strike breakers were both plentiful and cheap, for they were the unemployed. There had been a time, probably towards the end of the Depression in the late 1930's, when car ownership was the totem pole of the proud owner as it was in the U.K. in the 50's, 60's and 70's and, to some extent, still is. It quickly became a tool, necessary to anyone who lived more than walking distance from work, or went on vacation. The train network had all but vanished. Buses, except for the long distance Greyhound, used by only the very poor, non-existent. Nobody doubts that in the U.S.A. the car is more even than a tool, it is a prosthetic extension of the body. To be without one is a nightmare: unthinkable. How has this come about? The reasons are legion but here are a few. Cheap and plentiful oil, the genius of Henry Ford and others in the design and production of cars and trucks. The great distances between the towns which was O.K. when the train networks served the community, but when they went out of business the car became not just king, but a tyrant, and the car manufacturers saw nothing wrong with that.

In the 1940's there was a huge moral scandal in Los Angeles. L.A. possessed a very good local transport system, trams, buses and local trains. General Motors and the Firestone company conspired together, bought up the whole system and closed it down. That may have made economic sense but helped to destroy the cohesion of a very large community. Now, just think what will happen when America uses up all its own oil, and continuing trouble in the Middle East interrupts the steady flow to the U.S.A. America would go to war to get oil. Wars have been started for less. Remember the War for Jenkin's Ear against Spain in 1738?

So within quite a short time car possession became no big deal. They were cheap compared to those in Europe, and used cars very cheap indeed.

A favourite ploy of a group of students was to buy a used car in New York, drive it to California and dump it or sell it for what it might fetch, i.e., to a student group going from West to East. You had to be very low on the social scale to be without transport. Pride of ownership, except in such excellent examples of the designer's art as a Porsche, a Ferrari, or the cult cars such as the M.G. sports, was not great. There was also an attitude to ownership quite foreign to a European. Anybody who knew you would lend you his car. He would just toss you the keys. As to European cars generally, not many had been imported, partly because the European carmakers had not properly researched the market to determine what the Americans wanted in a car, partly because they were too small, looking like Dinky toys alongside the huge Fords, Cadillacs and Chevrolets, and poor reliability. British cars were poor on all counts, especially Jaguar which was fast approaching the nadir of quality. Electrical failure is usually responsible for 90% of car breakdowns and Lucas, the electrical supplier to just about the whole of the British car industry, was appalling. A witty Harvard don, on hearing yet again that a friend's Jaguar had broken down, said, "Ah! Lucas the Prince of Darkness, I suppose". In the U.K. cars tend to be nurtured and cosseted like a baby. Not so in the U.S.A. Benign neglect is more common where body condition is concerned. Their principal concern is with brakes, tyres and steering. I am in agreement with this.

A few years later on one of my yearly visits, my wife was with me, and we went for a few days to Martha's Vineyard, that delightful island off the coast of Connecticut, Summer playground of the wealthy. A young Bostonian in our hotel had a not very old car but with dents in it all over the place, I asked him if he had been in an accident. "No", he said, "It was done in a car park". It often happens in the U.S.A., people blocked in just bash their way out, using the bumper as a battering ram. On Martha's Vineyard it was a few years after the Teddy Kennedy incident, in which Kennedy, drunk, went over the edge of the small wooden bridge which connected Martha's Vineyard to another tiny island. The car turned over in fairly deep water. Kennedy managed to get out, but left behind the girl Mary Joe Kopechnic, his political aide. Back at the hotel at the water's edge, and in a terrible state of nerves, he called for help, but the girl was drowned. That destroyed Kennedy politically and he was never to be President as had his brother Jack. Within the next two days, the locals told us, over 400 journalists arrived on the island and thousands of gawkers. We drove over the bridge to the place where Kennedy was partying with his friends. The bridge looked brand new, and it was, because souvenir hunters over the ensuing months came over and hacked pieces out of the original until little was left.

Well! That was America, my first visit. A lesson in people and places, and a different way of life. Sometimes almost different languages, certainly many words spelt the same but with different meanings. Much to admire, and also something less than admirable. An open, generous and a strangely naïve, innocent people. It was not a country in which I could have lived comfortably, although many years later that was under serious discussion. But what I respected above all things was a level of democracy, of freedom, of liberty and a healthy criticism of big government which the U.K. falls far short of achieving.

A quotation from St. Matthew best sums up America, "For there is nothing covered that shall not be revealed; and hid, that shall not be known".

ITALY AND SWITZERLAND

IT IS NOT TRUE THAT IN WORLD WAR II

ITALIAN TANKS HAD THIRTEEN REVERSE GEARS

The Italians are a lightweight, frivolous people; at least that is the stereotype and received wisdom of Anglo Saxons. At first meeting they give that impression, but when regarded closer, especially in business matters, serious and penetrative are words that come to mind. They are subtle and clever at reading the important elements in a document, that which lies between the lines. They are family orientated to the point of lunacy and a relative, except in extreme cases, would be preferred to a non-family member, however good the latter may be. In the end it comes down to money, keeping it in the family, and secrecy. A family member will always be loyal; but a non-member? You can't always be sure. What other country has a tax police, La Garda Financia, in uniform? Who may stop you on the road for a chat, and a look in the boot for bags of cash, or uninvoiced goods on the way to a Swiss bank just over the border, which in the case of Lake Maggiore runs across the lake a few miles from Locarno? Now the Garda Financia has a Marine Section in very fast boats. Ernest Hemingway wrote a novel "The Sun also Rises" – the Italians have a cynical expression "The Nephew also Rises".

Italy in the 1950's by the standard of the UK was poor, with but a small middle class. But as a measure of their rapid upwards climb, the lira grew in value from 3,000 to the Pound in 1950 to 1,500 in the Pound in 1970. They never overtook us in living standard, as did the French, but by 1980 were breathing down our necks, even claiming that they were ahead of us in GNP (Gross National Product). Before 1960 I sold a lot of American and English equipment in Italy but by 1970 I was importing Italian made plant into the U.K. When a country's living standard improves an accurate sign is the importation of more food than is exported, especially luxury foods, and meat. Meat, especially beef, is a strong indicator of a country's wealth. Which is why one of the names given to the English by the French in the 19th century was "Rosbifs".

It is not widely known that the Italians under Mussolini built the first motor road in Europe, not the Germans. This was a short one, 15 miles from Naples to Pompeii, in 1930 and a little later another one, longer, from Milan to Lake Como. Both were built on motor road principles of which the most important was that no other road ran across it. Unhappily, at the time, and no doubt driven by lack of money, they were only 3 lane, hence overtaking at 100 mph was often done in the face of cars coming at the same speed from the opposite direction. Life on the Italian autostrada in the 1950's was always interesting, even if for some people rather short.

The great 4 lane highways, such as the Autostrada del Sole, from Milan to Naples and then on further South, were built at great speed and included feats of civil engineering unmatched anywhere in Europe. Between Bologna and Florence, a distance of about 55 miles, there are no fewer (and now I must guess although I have tried to count them many times) than 56 tunnels, some a mile long, and what are called "Galleria" which are roads sliced through a mountainside and roofed over. Such roads and structures are worthy of their Roman forebears and, rightly, you must pay to use them, as they are all toll roads. A country's attitude to paying its taxes is inversely proportional to its Government's need to charge for using its motorways. Thus, France and Italy are bitterly opposed to paying direct taxation, but pay heavily on their motoroads. The UK, Germany and Switzerland pay their direct taxation, but their motoroads are free.

As in France the centres of heavy industry are not well defined. Although industry in general is contained in the triangle of Milan – Turin – Genoa, there are small to medium sized towns all over the North in which industry developed outside of the influence of the great towns. And often the foundry, the oldest of all industries, became the epicentre of development. I have in mind Varese, Busto Assizio, Pavia, Lecco, Bergamo, Bologna and Brescia.

To the Milanese these places and their peoples are provincial rustics. To Milan even Rome is a place of lazy jobsworths, and Africa begins at

Naples. Why, they say, should the wealth of our hard work be siphoned off to support the lazy, improvident South? The male Milanese is almost Middle Eastern in the way he dresses his women in haute couture and showy jewelry as an outward and visible sign of his business success. Observe a Northern Italian going away for as little as a weekend and the number of expensive Louis Vuiton cases full of clothes taken for three days' wear. My single soft bag was often regarded with a barely concealed contempt.

Their attitude to the English is ambivalent but there is great respect for our political stability and probity in public life. They are not impressed by our lack of style, lack of panache and horrible food. Showing, of course, that their knowledge of us is just as innacurate as our knowledge of them. In one matter they admire us enormously, murders. The English murder to your average Italian *has* style. I recall in the late 1950's the Italian newspapers' excitement over Dr. Bodkin-Adams, the Eastbourne doctor. He had many wealthy widows as patients who gave him extravagant gifts, including a Rolls Royce, and some made him the sole beneficiary of their wills shortly before dying, with the good doctor holding a grateful hand. For weeks my Italian friends could talk of little else, and I half believed their readiness to cheer at his acquittal. Haigh, the acid bath murderer and Christie, of the Notting Hill murders, were equally popular.

In my peripatetical Italian wanderings between 1956 and 1996 two events are deep in my memory. One is hilarious and bizarre and the other dramatic. On a Sunday, when staying at the Milan home of Angelo our Italian agent and his wife Flora, he suggested, and Flora agreed, that he took me to see something perhaps strange to the eyes of a Brit. It could have been Paris at the end of the 19th century rather than Milan in the middle of the 20th. He took me to a large 18th century mansion, in a large and well-kept garden, with a splendid Palladian entrance. A maid opened the door, and with a smile led us into an elegant drawing room with well dressed men seated, talking to extremely beautiful women. It took about a nanno-second to grasp. I was in a bordello, a knocking shop, and there was Angelo looking at my face and peeing himself with laughter. Madam sat behind a handsome desk and there were two carved, baroque staircases leading to the rooms above, one to the left up which a gentleman with his choice of lady walked, arm in arm, and one to the right down which a lady and her partner walked arm in arm. At the bottom the lady gave an envelope to Madam and the gentleman departed. It was so discreet, so stylish, so Italian. This was no Texas whorehouse.

And now for the drama. Angelo had a Maserati sports car of which he was immensely proud, and which finally killed him. He was a highly skilled driver with whom I loved to be a passenger, and absolutely safe. One morning he came down to find his car missing, stolen. A car of that distinction usually ended up in Hungary or Romania, said the police, and Angelo had to be reconciled to its permanent loss. He had a nephew, Amanda, not much younger than Angelo because he was a late offspring of Angelo's oldest sister, of whom he had four. Amanda was about thirty-two to my thirty-eight and Angelo's forty-two. Now Amanda has a Swiss girlfriend of many years living in Lugano just over the border. Like many an Irishman of his age, he was shy, positively frightened of marriage, and lived a comfortable life with his mother, and sold J & B scotch whisky in the North area. She liked it, he liked it, but his girlfriend hated it. Still, there you go, La Dolce Vita. About three weeks after the theft, Amanda was going to Lugano and asked if I would like to go with him. Why not, it was a fine day, the route alongside Lake Como was beautiful and Lugano an attractive Swiss town? So off we went. We were on the edge of Lugano when suddenly he shouted, "Look! There's Angelo's car". It was parked outside a smart restaurant and we parked close behind, bumper to bumper, so that it was blocked in. There was an open air café next to the restaurant in which we sat and waited. In about 30 minutes a young bloke came out of the restaurant, went to the car, put his hand on the door and Amanda was on him like a charging bull, me by his side. We had him. There was a lot of noise, and somebody phoned the Swiss police who responded quickly. The Swiss hate criminals who stole things from hard working Swiss burghers. After a quick call to Angelo he was with us in a couple of hours, along with proof of ownership, etc., and in two days he was a proud owner again.

To most Italians, food is of the commanding heights, as it is to the French, but it is extraordinarily regional. In the Venato it differs greatly from Lombardy, and in Tuscany is as different again. The Italian, as a commodity does not export too well. He loves his country too much and, in my experience, finds it difficult to cope not only with foreign food, but also with food from the wrong part of Italy, i.e., not his part. Once I had two Italian engineers in the UK doing a large installation job, and I was quite distraught, for they could not handle British food. The idea of a fried breakfast almost made them sick. Until I found an Italian restaurant, not easy in Walsall, they would only eat bread, and drink red wine. They were from the Veneto which contains such splendid towns as Verona, Vicenza and Padua, and whose food suits me very well. Frankly, I am happier with Italian cuisine than French. Its simplicity is appealing and most Italian restaurants offer few menu changes, and dishes for which the microwave oven is never used. Remember, the great cuisine of France had its home originally in Italy at the courts of the Medici, Orsini and other great 15th century families.

But one dish I found hard to handle. A great delicacy in the North is "Vicelli con Polenta". "Vicelli" means bird and "Polenta" is that staple of the North, sometimes more so than pasta, made from maize. The first time I had it there were six small birds roasted, complete with beaks, speared on a skewer and served on a bed of polenta. I was stunned. "What birds?" I said, "Any birds" said the waiter. I ate them suffused with guilt.

My American boss, Herbert von Wolff, mostly I think to escape company headquarters in Cleveland, came to see me three times a year, thankfully only for about four or five days. An Austrian by birth and a sensitive man he knew when I'd had enough. He liked Italy where he could meet Flora, his youngest sister, wife of Angelo our Italian agent. In the Spring of 1962 I was to meet him at Linate Airport, Milan from whence we were to motor to Zurich and then back to Milan. His time of arrival was about 1330 hours but before then I had to go to Bologna to inspect equipment that had arrived the previous day. It was a round trip about 350 miles and eight hours so I left Milan at 0500 hours. I was back at Linate just in time to greet him.

Now I must digress somewhat. Four weeks earlier I had taken delivery of a new Austin 110. It was a new model with a straight six-cylinder engine, supposedly a competitor for BMW. At its launch Austin, greatly proud, announced they were seeking one hundred people to test it thoroughly over an extended period. Ever willing to give my old engineering alma mater a leg up and Austin Co. was also a customer, I went to the Managing Director of Sales who, like most of Austin's senior management, was an ex-Austin apprentice and suggested I should be one of the lucky one hundred. How naïve can you get? "You are the last sort of driver we want. We want people who will use the car for driving to work, and perhaps, take the wife and kids for a spin during the weekend. Not a madman who will drive it at 100mph on German motor roads, and up and down Swiss mountain passes. " You live and learn.

Wolff and I left Milan at about 1500 hours and I had now motored 350 miles since 0500. The route to Zurich was Como, Lugano, Bellinzona, the St. Gothard Pass (6,000 feet), the Süsten Pass (7,230 feet), the Brüning Pass (3,500 feet) to Luzern. From there it was more or less downhill to Zurich. With a bit of luck we would be in Zurich by 2000 hours. "A piece of cake", I thought. The weather was fine and all the Passes we had to traverse were open and free of snow. We were delayed a little at the Süsten Pass owing to a small avalanche that required clearing. The sort of thing the Swiss handle swiftly. Thereafter it was easy until the downhill run to Luzern. It was now twilight and going down the mountain all the lights failed About a mile short of the town, now in complete darkness, there was a smell of burning and smoke was pouring from the bonnet. I stopped, opened the bonnet and ripped out the leads of the battery. It was now about nine o'clock and we sat and thought for a bit. Suddenly, out of the gloom, I heard a voice, "I can see you are in trouble, can I help?" it said. So I told the tale once more as I had become accustomed to it in my job. He spoke English but anyway Wolff spoke German, his native tongue. "Look" the man said, "I have a large garage and car distributorship a few hundred metres from here. Give me your keys, the last train to Zurich goes in 20 minutes and I'll run you to the station. Come back in three days and I will have replaced all the wiring, if necessary." I had now been awake since 0430, driven 800 miles over three mountain passes and I then gave the keys of a brand new car to a complete stranger who said he could do the repair in three days. You couldn't make it up. Sighs of relief all round. After all, it was Switzerland, not Ireland. In Zurich we could not find a room, several conferences had claimed all the hotels and we drove round in a taxi for an hour but had no luck. So back to the station we went, bought sandwiches and beer, and slept, if you could call it that, in a waiting room. At midnight my day had now extended to 20 hours long. At about 6 o'clock next morning we washed, shaved and had breakfast, feeling remarkably fresh. "Wait until tonight" said Wolff, "when it all catches up with you".

Our Swiss agent's office was only a few hundred yards from the station and we were with him at 07.30. Three days later we went to our benefactor in Luzern to see a washed car ready for us to drive away. Most people are happy to be in Switzerland, but some have reservations about the Swiss. I have none for it was not the first time I had received marvellous service and good manners there. The cost was £50, not bad for 1962. I would have paid £500, or at least my boss would have. How can you put a price on such kindness as that Swiss gentleman (I can call him no less) showed to us? It took twelve months to get compensation out of Austin. In those days a warrantee was what the car manufacturer said it was. They deserved to go broke and I was glad when they did.

During the Suez War in September 1956 when the Israelis, in collusion with the British and French, attacked Egypt, the Middle East Arab oil producers turned the tap off and we had petrol rationing. Coupons were issued and a black market soon developed. "Just like the War", said some of the old folks with a smile of satisfaction on their faces.

A nifty little gadget was being offered which, if attached to a carburettor, claimed to reduce petrol consumption by 20%. It did this by thinning the petrol mix. My garage fitted one for me, and off I went to Italy via the Simplon Pass in Switzerland. It seemed to work on long, straight, flat roads in France, petrol usage was clearly down. At Brig, I started the climb to Simplon, but when I was up to about 1,500 feet the radiator was boiling and I had no choice but to go down for water. The road was narrow and it was impossible to turn round, with a very steep drop on one side. Believe it or not I had to go backwards for several hundred yards before there was room to turn round. Nearly at the bottom there was a house that gave me water and I set off up the mountain again. At the same spot, again the radiator boiled, and again I went backwards before being able to turn round. I was now a bag of nerves. This time, and having allowed the engine to cool, I drove to a repair garage quite near, in Brig. A mechanic took one look at the carburettor, laughed, and said he had removed several of those gadgets in the last month. The problem was height. Above about 1,500 feet where the air was thinner it didn't work and I was off again. There may be people who drive as well backwards as forwards. There may be people who *prefer* to drive backwards. I am not one of them.

Colin Gillespie, a friend of mine, was one of the leaders of the English revival of commercial winegrowers in the early 1970's. He had about five acres of vineyard on a lovely, idyllic site at North Wootton, near Wells in Somerset. Unusually he was both a skilled grower and a good wine maker. This is a happy combination for a good wine maker can save a bad harvest, but a poor wine maker can ruin a good one. Colin's white wine, made from several different varieties of grape but mainly Müller Thurgau, could stand proudly in the presence of very great whites from countries of long tradition in the viticulture craft. In another chapter you will learn of the respect given to his wine by German growers.

Sometime in 1984 I was having a drink at his vineyard, well, several actually, and in the long and bibulous conversation that followed, he just happened to mention that he had two cases of wine to deliver to the British Ambassador at the UN in Geneva and was at a loss how to deliver such a small amount at a reasonable transport cost. He is a cunning old bastard and later I decided he had always intended to bring up the subject with me, guessing what my re-action would be. "No problem", I said, or probably shouted, "I shall be near Geneva in a couple of weeks and I'll drop them off". How near is near? Is 100 miles near? Because that was the detour made to deliver those two cases of wine. For once I had taken my wife with me, as she had never seen Geneva, or Vienna, which was our final destination.

It was dusk when we reached Geneva but the Ambassador's residence was easily found. The door was opened by a tall cadaverous man who said he was Jack, the Ambassador's valet. He took the wine saying his master was out but would be in tomorrow morning if I wished to see him but we needed to leave early, so that was that. The job was done and Colin would be pleased. A lovely day dawned, warm and sunny, which was just and well, for when we were clear of the lakeside and on the main road to Lausanne, what should we see ahead but a long haired, black bearded man in heavy black boots, heel and toeing it, elbows pumping away, and stark bollock naked. Later I wished I had stopped to ask where he was heading and offered him a lift. As I said, it was warm, a good day for a stroll in the altogether.

In November 1963, after two weeks in Serbia, Belgrade and a boghole called Kikinda, up near the Rumanian border, plus a week in Italy, I wanted to get home – quick. So I left Milan rather late, about 4 o'clock. I took the usual route (if I had had a donkey, he would have known the route better than I), SestoCalende and Domodossola, to begin the steep climb to the Simplon Pass (6,800 feet). The roads to the mountains and on the mountains were still poor. It was already middle November and I was surprised the Pass was still open. At the top I got out of the car and lit a cigarette. There was the silence of the grave. I could hear the car settling on its springs, the water trickling from the radiator into the motor block and the cylinder head. It was so quiet that if two people one hundred yards away had been talking normally they would have been heard. I was absolutely alone. No cars coming from Switzerland and none from Italy. The temperature must have been about −10°, and just as I was getting back into my car a few flakes of snow touched my face. In 45 minutes I was down the mountain and snug in my Brig hotel. Next morning as I departed at about 7 o'clock, I was told the Pass was closed and would remain so until late March. I had crossed over the night before with about an hour to spare.

It was a hard drive but the 650 miles were comfortably done and I arrived at Dunkirk at 8 o'clock. In the railway station I sat down to a splendid dinner of steak au poivre, a litre of beer and a large piece of cheese and bread, not having eaten since breakfast. A feature of those days was the splendid food to be had in the railway stations of France and Switzerland, notably Basle, Zurich, Dunkirk and Lyon. I have had countless dinners in those places at the end of a day's long hard drive. After eating I drove down to the docks on to the deck of the rustbucket which British Rail put on for the winter trade which was very light. About six cars could be placed across the deck. It was not strictly a car ferry. Departure was at midnight so I went down to the saloon for a kip. At about 5 o'clock noise and voices told me we were at, or near, Dover. On deck, to my astonishment, mine was the only car and there were no foot passengers. Awaiting me and my car was a small army of Customs and Excise, cleaners and other people. It was a right royal reception and one or two of them even managed a smile. I was home by 7.30, and didn't leave the country for another six months. It was hard staying at home.

Next day Jack Kennedy was assassinated.

GERMANY

GOETHE SAID OF HIS COUNTRYMEN

"THEY ARE A STRANGE MIXTURE OF MUSIC AND MURDER".

I have three strong mental pictures of Germany. The first is of flying over the Ruhr some months after the end of World War II and seeing for the first time the cataclysmic destruction of many towns, including Dusseldorf. It was as though a gigantic steel cable had encircled thousands of square miles and pulled the top storey off every building. The second seems worse. Dietrich Bonhoeffer, a young Lutheran pastor, was hanged after being two years in Buchenwald Concentration Camp, a few days before the end of the War. His crime? He tried to form a link between the Germans opposed to Hitler and the British Government. The third is of that exquisite choral work of Beethoven at the end of the 9th Symphony, "The Ode to Spring". Goethe did indeed know his countrymen

The devastation of war, greater even than in Russia, the death of millions, not counting the five millions in the Holocaust, the almost total destruction of the industrial base, its housing base, leaving nowhere for its work force to live. Those disasters the Germans started to repair with quite exceptional energy and speed. So that when I went there first on business in 1955, business, especially heavy industry, was working flat out, the hotels were decent, and tourists were plentiful, despite tens of thousands living in conditions not far removed from holes in the ground. At a guess, I would say conditions were already better only ten years away from the end of the War than was Russia or its satellites fortyfive years after the War. The Germans are truly remarkable. Among my German friends, and I still have plenty, the more sardonic occasionally posed the rhetorical question "How come the greatest military race since the Romans, the best educated people, the greatest industrial force, the hardest working, be defeated in two World Wars by the bumbling, amateurish British, who always leave everything to the last minute?" I could have told them but never did.

It was weird, if pleasing, how little resentment they bore against the English (as in France, we were generally referred to by the Germans as "the English", rather than "the British") They also referred to us as "Tommys". Hamburg received considerable attention from the RAF in the period 1941-2-3, but one raid stands out in the minds of those who survived the demon's night in 1942 when 30,000 were killed, NOT from high explosive but fire and suffocation. The fire was so fierce it sucked all the oxygen out of the air so that there was none left to breathe. As one Hamburgian said to me wryly, "We dropped the bill on London, you dropped the payment on us." It was rare to be at the unpleasant end of resentment over the War when in Germany. It was much more common in France – our Allies.

A good stroke of luck was my choice of agent. Peter Edler and I met in September 1956 and hit it off immediately. Ten years younger but widely experienced in some of life's nastier surprises. Such as, at the age of fourteen in 1945, having a rifle thrust into his hand as part of a youth defence battalion to fight amongst the ruins of Dusseldorf. Together for many years, we travelled to the great industrial centres of the Ruhr, Hanover, Hamburg, Bremen, Mannheim and Munich; in the foundries of BMW, Daimler-Benz (Mercedes), Volkswagen, Ford and many more. Even then what remained of German industry was much bigger than that of the U.K.

Edler's family had been part of the huge Mannesmann industrial group and, at barely twenty, he was given the pleasant but tiring job of entertaining visiting customers, mostly between the hours of 10pm and 3am in the restaurants and highly entertaining and classy Dusseldorf strip clubs. Many of the metropolitan German towns had similar establishments but in Dusseldorf there was a distinct whiff of 1930's Berlin in the places and performers; that's what I was told by some of the old goats of the period. Everybody knew Peter and although in 1956 he was no longer engaged in such "man about town" activity he was still remembered. We would go into one place and the Maitre d' would see him and come over with a glass of champagne – "How are you Peter? What are you up to now?", and in another "Good Evening Herr Edler, how are you?" And so on, all over Dusseldorf, not to mention Munich and Frankfort.

Between 1956 and 1980 I learnt more about Germany than I ever knew about the UK, in the travel sense that is, mountains, rivers, towns, medieval cities, walled villages, gambling in Baden-Baden, vineyards of the Rheinpfalz, Rheinhessen, the Rheingau, Baden, Mosel and Franconia. We made two visits only to the Eastern Zone. Peter had been at school in Zwickau about 50 miles South of Leipzig and wanted to visit it after Leipzig, which was our primary target, for an International Exhibition. Leipzig and Hanover were the oldest exhibition towns in the world. The secondary reason was personal. Peter had a very old uncle living there in poor conditions, in two rooms with several dependents, and he was wondering what to take them as a useful present. He had a brilliant idea, a crate of oranges, one of those wooden boxes commonplace in greengrocers years ago. It was about 30" high and 18" in diameter with open slatted sides. At the frontier a stony faced guard grinned broadly when given a couple, and said he had not seen an orange for more than twelve months. That, in 1970, summed up the difference between West and East Germany. The uncle, an old soldier from World War I and an active General in WW II, was beside himself with joy and whipped out a bottle of brandy being kept for a special occasion. What could be better than to celebrate the arrival of, perhaps, the only oranges in Leipzig? Between the frontier and Leipzig all roads off the main road were guarded. No visitors were permitted to move off the main route. We never saw Peter's school and had to return exactly on the arrival route. The police would not let us move around.

The relief on re-entering the West near Erfurt was like coming home after a trying visit to an unpleasant place. When, years later, a few months after the Berlin Wall was pulled down in November 1989, I went by train from Hamburg to Berlin, a distance of 200 miles through the Eastern Zone. There was such industrial squalor and pollution, such dilapidation of housing, farms and towns. How, I puzzled, could a country, even one so divided by a political and physical barrier, be as different as chalk from cheese after only 44 years? Truly, democracy must have something special which is denied to socialism.

In the 1950's there was a strange omission in all German hotels, save the 4 star variety – soap. There was no shortage in the shops, but in the hotels you brought your own. This continued into the 1960's and I never found out why, despite the rapid recovery from shortages (we still had some food rationing years after it had ceased in Germany). There was a delightful sense of an earlier age, almost like the Edwardian England of Jerome K. Jerome when he wrote "Three Men in a Boat". In villages in Bavaria or the Pfalz Palatinate near Heidelberg where I often stayed, there would be a Gasthaus with, perhaps, six rooms and a bar cum restaurant, clean and comfortable with no bathroom but plenty of hot water and tap water that tasted good. In the bar there would be probably a single or perhaps two long scrubbed plain tables where you would eat, and drink the beer which may have been brewed in the village, alongside der Herr Docktor, der Herr Schulmeister and der Herr Burgomeister. The room in sterling may have been £3, but the dinner perhaps the same or more, for food in Germany cost more then than in the UK. When we joined the Common Market in 1972 everything changed and the reverse was true. Today you can still eat better and cheaper than in the UK.

Until 1965 German industry worked very long hours. They needed to do so to keep up with the requirements of the home market and even more for exports. Direct taxation was high but lower than ours, but deductions from the wage packet for state pensions and health were huge, to pay for the health service, which in association with some private contribution, givens them health care greatly superior to our own. With no stroppy, politically motivated unions and an educated work force and managerial class, they had outstripped our living standard by 1960.

There was an odd eccentricity in the workshop, which must have had its origins years earlier. Certainly up to 1970, if you went into one at about 8 o'clock when the workers on the 0600 to 1400 hours shift stopped for breakfast, either at their benches or in the canteen, the table would be loaded with bottles of beer, cigarettes and, sometimes, a bottle of cognac. There were also dispensing machines for beer.

From 1956 onwards, most months found me on the German motoroads involved in putting UK and American built machines into German foundries. By 1965 when our manufacturing base of capital equipment was already being eroded by union activity, low production, poor quality and high prices, I was importing German equipment to replace that hitherto built by UK companies, but forced into liquidation by a combination of the reasons just stated. My German principal, whose equipment I was importing, had its manufacturing plant in the small and beautiful baroque town of Schwetzingen, about five miles from Heidelberg. For over 30 years I stayed there four or five times each year, often in the same hotel. Sometimes the babies born in the early 1960's, whom I knew, were serving me in the 1980's. How pleasant it was to stay in a hotel owned by the same family for some generations.

The Germans can be very irritating, and frequently quite bizarre in their attitude towards the letter, rather than the spirit of the law. The are inclined to write things down. A business letter will be signed by two people (safety in numbers?). It has been said that the reason the Israelis were able to hang Eichman and the other monsters who administered what was called The Final Solution (it sounds better than murder) of the Jews, was their obsession with recording in writing everything done. E.g. "Yesterday May 14th, despatched two trainloads of workers to Auschwitz. Had lunch with Heidi and our little son Siegfried. He looked so innocent in his new sailor suit."

Every time I neared Munich on the motoroad I saw the signpost "Dachau – 17km". This concentration camp opened in 1933, one month after Hitler came to power. It was not an extermination camp at first, but a place of punishment for political dissidents, trade union leaders, Free Masons, and anyone that couldn't keep his mouth shut. After several years of looking at this sign, and it was a Saturday morning when I had some time on my hands, I went to Dachau. Not many people were there but they were mostly Germans. It is not something I want to dwell on too much, except to be there was a million times more awful than seeing it on television. The whipping stools, the gallows, the gas ovens, the bunks for 3,000 which later served 6,000, two to a bunk, but the worst of all that was to be seen were the huge blown up pictures, ten feet high by twenty feet long, of the train on to which men, women and children were being marshalled, while groups of German soldiers were standing by laughing between themselves. Laughing? Why were they laughing?

I could bear it no longer and left to spend the night in Salzburg before pushing on next day to Czechoslovakia.

I got very drunk that night in Salzburg

One evening, after a late night party with some friends in the small town of Giessen, walking to my hotel at about midnight on deserted roads, I came to a set of traffic lights. There were three people waiting to cross but the light was at red. With no cars in sight I walked across. Then I noticed the group of three had not followed. Curious, I waited to see when they would move. After about two minutes, the light turned to green and so they came across. Very odd, don't you think? Great respecters of the law.

In the Winter of 1961 I was engaged on a large project at the Volkswagen works at Wolfsberg, a new town built by the company near the East/West border, near to Hannover. Through carelessness on my part I was struck on the head by a descending part of a large machine. Out of the corner of my eye I saw it coming and received only a glancing blow, otherwise I would have been killed. I staggered to my feet with blood streaming down my face, and the first thing that was said to me was "Are you insured?" *not* "Are you O.K.?" In the First Aid Room the nurse said "Are you insured?". Then the doctor came and, before stitching my scalp HE said, "Are you insured?" The Germans have a strange sense of priorities – and I wasn't insured.

One day in 1944 while looting a small deserted and happily unboobytrapped castello in Tuscany, I came across several dozen bottles of red wine, handsomely boxed in wood. Clearly this was not rubbish. My mess was very pleased and a brother officer, professional wine taster to a lordly and ancient London house of wine importers, gasped when he read a label. I had "liberated", for that was the term used, three cases of Chateau Lafite 1937, the greatest red grown in Bordeaux, of one of the greatest vintages of the century thus far. That was my first experience of drinking a wine that none but the wealthy could afford. This was no Chianti rubbish. That was a seminal moment which set me on to an interest in wine which has never left me, and because of my somewhat unorthodox life allowed me to indulge myself amidst half the vineyards of Europe. Later I wrote about wine in several wine journals, and even planted a tiny vineyard on my property to, as it were, put my money where my mouth was. This venture into the life of the vigneron taught me a major truth. The only people who make money out of wine are the makers of the bottles, the corks and the labels.

There is, believe it or not, an English wine business. By that I mean there are people who have planted vineyards, harvest grapes and make wine, on a total of about 2,000 acres and on a line roughly below the Wash to the Severn. Among the growers, either professional or semi-professional, there are a small elite who make white wine which can stand without shame among some of the finest whites grown in Europe. Because I knew and liked many of the growers, and was in an unique position to give their wines publicity, I wrote about their efforts and managed to plant articles in various European journals including Die Weldt and other newspapers. Of course, it was a great laugh to the Germans and the French "Wine from England? What date is it, April lst?" I also wrote to several Ambassadors suggesting it might help the fledgling English industry if they were to serve English wine at Embassy functions. Cheek can often succeed and it worked. In 1978, the Silver Anniversary of Her Majesty's reign, I wrote to Sir Oliver Wright, the British Ambassador at Bonn, the German capital (in the absence of Berlin). He replied personally and ordered 25 cases of English Muller Thurgau, grown and made by my old friend Major Colin Gillespie at North Wootton, near Wells in Somerset. At a later date it was some of his wine I delivered to the British Ambassador to the U.N. in Geneva, of which I wrote in the chapter on Italy and Switzerland.

Sir Oliver, knowing I travelled a lot in Germany, asked me to lunch. Two months later I arrived at the Residency, the Ambassador's house on the Rhein just outside Bonn, expecting to be just one of a gathering of British businessmen having lunch with the Ambassador, but no, it was just Lady Wright, Sir Oliver and me. A minor skill I have is the ability to recall conversations or written articles, heard or read, some years before. In 1968 when the troubles in Ulster had reached a peak, and it was decided to suspend the Ulster Parliament and govern from Whitehall, two Foreign Office officials were sent to Belfast to administer Ulster. One of the couple was a Mr. Oliver Wright. He was delighted that I knew and remembered, they always are. "Why did they send you and the other man?" I asked. He laughed and said they were the only chaps not on leave. That I thought is the way the English do it.

The ice was, from that point, nicely broken, and it became the most memorable three hour luncheon in a fairly long experience of luncheons; a well bred Riesling from the Rheingau to Remy Martin cognac and Havana cigars. I can't remember the food, except that it slotted well into the wine.

He then told me a story connected with the wine I had sold him. A few years earlier he had had his first posting to Bonn as First Secretary. Earlier this year during a TV programme in Berlin he was asked what changes he had observed compared with his previous tour. "Well, " he replied, "I have a feeling I enjoyed German wine rather more then than now, but I may be wrong." There was uproar in the daily newspapers, headlines such as "English Ambassador scorns our wines". The upshot was the Embassy was flooded with cases of wine from anxious growers from all over Germany.

To mollify these anxious growers, he gave a luncheon attended by a fair gathering of them at which, and unknown to them, he served my friend Colin's Muller Thurgau. They were fulsome with their praise, and recognised the grape but were puzzled. Muller Thurgau is a very common grape in Germany making wines of middling character, not like the one they were drinking. Then he teased them to identify the wine's provenance. From this place, said one, no, from that place said another, and so it went on. Then they begged him to tell. So he did. Momentarily they were stunned and wouldn't believe him until he showed them the label. But they continued to praise it while saying it was nearly as good as their own wines. Honour was satisfied all round. What they did not know was the Muller Thurgau from reasons of climate and growing conditions, and in the right hands, will always make a better wine in England than anywhere else. We then talked politics ranging far and wide, and for a diplomat, Sir Oliver Wright was remarkably frank, especially about politicians of all political colours. The Government of the time was the Socialists under Callaghan. One of Wilson's Foreign Secretaries had been George Brown, poor drunken insecure George. Everybody loved him, especially the Foreign Office, or so the papers said. "Was that true?" I asked. "Yes" said Sir Oliver. "Why?" I asked. "Because he always did as he was told" said Sir Oliver.

After Germany Sir Oliver Wright became the British Ambassador at Washington.

THE LEVANT

I use the old fashioned term for those countries whose coastlines form the Eastern Mediterranean. It is more accurate than "Near East" which was often used up to 1939, but has now been replaced by "Middle East", or, if one is American, "Mid-East", since Americans find "Middle East" difficult to pronounce. To me the very word "Levant" summons up the Biblical vista as the seat of all ancient history, and the smells of spice markets, passing camels, and the muezzin calling the Faithful to prayer from the mosque minaret. To your sturdy Englishman of the 19th and early 20th centuries, bound hand and foot by his xenophobia, often learnt from the novels of such authors as John Buchan, G. K. Chesterton and the author of Bulldog Drummond novels, "Sapper", the term "greasy Levantine" sprang readily from his lips.

The racial, religious and geographical groupings were surely the most polyglot on earth. Greeks were in Egypt, Southern Turkey, Syria and the Lebanon. Egyptians were in the Lebanon, Syria and Palestine and the Jews were everywhere. Catholics, Greek Orthodox, Russian Orthodox, Armenians, Copts and Maronites all professed to be Christians and all quarreled over doctrine and religious interpretation of the Gospels. Athanasius and the Council of Nicaea of 325 A.D. have much to answer for. Christian, Jew and Arab lived cheek by jowl more or less in amity for hundreds of years. How different it is today.

The Levant was a place constantly in my mind for many years. I knew little of it even though the requirements of war put me in Egypt and Libya between 1939 and 1945. I was only briefly in Palestine. So I suggested to my American employers in May 1961 that I spent a few weeks in Greece, Turkey, Israel and Egypt in pursuit of trade, especially for the future. "Go, by all means, if you think it worth while. Go, research and make contact." That is the support and freedom of action that all salesmen dream about but which is rarely granted. Certainly few British firms of the time would have let me loose in such a manner without a guarantee of success.

A lot of research was necessary in London in the planning and preparation. Visits to embassies, meetings with trade attachés, who can be quite useful if they do their jobs properly, and various other avenues needed to be explored in order to build up a dossier that would gain entry into the foundry industries in the four countries I wanted to visit during the month of July. A fair amount of the information was out of date, which is always the way, but much of it was reliable and a useful package of industrial intelligence was put together. Appointments made by letter and telex assured me entrance to many foundries and trade associations before my departure on July 1st. To b e going near, if not exactly in, the footsteps of St. Paul gave one a distinct frisson of excitement.

There remained a singularly unusual problem, passports. Arab states would not allow entry to anyone carrying a passport bearing evidence that it had been used in Israel. Surprisingly, this was easily dealt with and the Passport Office in Petit France Street issued an additional one for use when going to Israel. I now carried my normal passport consisting of three stuck together. Reason? Every time a visit was made to an Iron Curtain country a visa had to be bought and stuck into the passport with a photograph. A visa occupied a full page and with about 20 visit a year to Czechoslovakia and the others, a passport was soon filled up. This took about eighteen months, but a passport life was seven years. Hence the sticking of them together. Four passports in a pocket could ruin a well cut suit, and with about eight different currencies stuffed into other pockets more damage was done. Why different currencies you may ask? Principally because when I was free the banks were shut and foreign banks in those days were ball achingly bureaucratic and money changing could be a major time consuming operation. For the same reason I never carried traveller's cheques

July in the Levant is not a month normally recommended for a business trip but beggars can't be choosers. In August most of Europe shuts down for the annual holiday. Indeed, in much of France so do the restaurants and shops (or, rather, used to, not now of course) and you could be on the edge of starvation should you be marooned in Paris in August. Very strange, since Paris is usually full of tourists in that month. But July it had to be, because from September onwards I had appointments elsewhere. Travel also was going to be fearsomely complicated, for not only was there a passport problem, but travel from a Muslim state to Israel was not allowed: or from Israel to a Muslim state. Moreover a single airline could not issue a single ticket covering all legs of the total journey. This was the passport problem writ large. Somebody of a clerkly bent was needed to deal with such affairs and, though not good at it, years of dealing with totalitarian bureaucracies had taught me a certain rough clerical skill. So the route finally worked out was: London – Athens – Istanbul – Beirut – Cairo – Athens – Tel Aviv – London. Until the mid-80's there was not a lot of mass air travel and certainly no cheap tickets. In comparison with today

Travelling by air was very, very expensive. One advantage, though, was absolute flexibility of tickets. If you missed a flight you could catch another, and without penalty. Moreover, the major airlines would accept each other's tickets.

Greece

Athens gave a first impression of being greatly distant from Western Europe, and the further you moved through Greece into what was really a sector of the Balkans, the more remote Paris or London or Rome seemed. The old Turkish Ottoman Empire came to mind. Everybody seemed to be moving in slow motion. Athens was a classic example of the poor country in which vast numbers, remote from the capital, were convinced that its streets were paved with gold and all you had to do was go there and dig some up. The result of this was that half of the eight million population of Greece was squeezed into Athens together with 90% of the cars in the country. Greece verged on being a third world state, there not apparently being a second world state. Why not? The production of daily newspapers did seem to be very modern as to the number of titles available and the number of readers. I was told, and since I knew only two words of Greek, kaliniko and kalisperos, the teller might have been moved by malice, that general conversation verged on the infantile, rivalling the Italians, and that I DO understand. But in laidbackness taking it easy, tomorrow is another day lifestyle, they were to be admired. By U.K. attitudes they were to be envied. They had none of the Anglo Saxon get-up-and-goism

A typical scene as you strolled down Vass Georgiou Street, or in Syntagmas Square, wherein lay my hotel the Grande Bretagne, was of cafés crowded with men, drinking Turkish coffee and fingering their strings of worry beads. Of course, you must not ask for Turkish coffee lest the waiter spit in it, or worse, but Greek. The enmity, the naked hatred of Greek for Turk can be measured in centuries. But now it is probably worse than during the latter part of the Turkish occupation. The Turks left in about 1850 but had been there for the previous four hundred years. They had lived reasonably together between Independence and 1920, and there were sizeable Greek communities in Constantinople, as Istanbul was then called, and on the Mediterranean coast around Smyrna, now Izmir. In fact, they had been in Turkey and Asia Minor for three millennia.

The Turks had always been tolerant of different cultures and religions, but political dissidence was punished with condign savagery. However, in 1920 – 1922 the Greeks chanced their arm against Turkey weakened, as they thought, by being on the wrong side in the Great War of 1914 – 1918, and attacked East across the Anatolian Plain. This was a great error for the Turks were not Italians. The Greeks were pushed back, literally, into the sea near Smyrna. Men, Women and children were massacred. It was Kemal Attaturk, the reforming modernising Turk who did it. He who banned the fez, the veil and changed the alphabet from Arabic to the Latin. That is why you must never ask for Turkish coffee in Greece.

Athens, like Venice, is a city to be visited at least once before shuffling off this mortal coil. Not for the shabby, ramshackle town of the 19th and 20th centuries but for the Acropolis Hill and the Parthenon which stands upon it, and has done since the great Pericles built it and the Erechthium in the years following 450 BC If you come out of Syntagma Square and turn left on Vass Georgiou Street, and walk in the direction of Omonia Square, down every turning on the left you will see the Acropolis and the glorious architecture upon it. It is quite creepy, like being followed by the eyes of the Mona Lisa in the Louvre. On my first morning I got up at five o'clock, with the day still wearing a little residual heat from the hot night, and the dawn just breaking, and walked the few hundred yards to the Acropolis. Alone, absolutely alone, I stayed for nearly two hours and was still alone when the sun was fully above the horizon. That was a princely way to see a part of "The Glory that was Greece". You couldn't do it today, the whole site is locked and barred at nightfall.

Another distinguishing feature of Athens was a practice not seen in London or Paris for a hundred years or more. In the centre were streets named, in Greek of course, Cobblers' Street, Plumbers' Street, Painting and Decorating Street and others. Each was devoted entirely to an artisan trade, with the artisans standing, complete with tools, waiting to be hired.

Greece was so poor, wages so low and industrialisation so underdeveloped, perhaps at the level of the U.K. in 1900, that the chances of business of the sort that was making the West hum and living standards rapidly improve, were not good. I was at least ten years too soon. I should have returned in 1975 but never did.

Turkey

After seven days in Greece, the eighth day found me over Turkey, looking down on the Dardanelles, scene of the ghastly Gallipoli campaign in April 1913. Churchill had the brilliant idea of striking at Constantinople as it was then called, the "soft underbelly" of the Central Powers. This consisted of landing a strong naval assault at the tip of the Gallipoli Peninsular and then moving north to take Constantinople from the south west and link up with the Russians. This would destroy the Ottoman Empire in the Arabian Peninsular, Mesopotamia, Palestine, Syria and The Lebanon, and then leave the half million British and Allied troops tied down there available to join the slaughterhouse of the Western Front in France.

Bad planning, bad leadership and bad luck provided another half million dead and wounded, made up of British, French, Australian and New Zealand soldiers and, of course, the Turks who were the victors. The bad luck came from a certain Mustafa Kemal Attaturk who guessed the Allied battle plans correctly. He went on to greater things and

Winston Churchill, the chief can holder, was disgraced. Twentyfour years elapsed before his country called on his services again at the age of 65, and we all know about that.

Clearly to be seen from about 5000 feet, and perhaps 30 minutes from Istanbul (as Constantinople had been renamed) was the Hellespont, the setting for the legend of Hero and Leander who swam nightly across the Hellespont to meet his lover. Throughout ancient history it was the passage from Asia Minor to Europe at its narrowest point. King Xerxes of Persia crossed the strait on a bridge of boats in 1481BC on his was to defeating the Greeks at the pass of Thermopylae. Though better remembered than he is Leonidas and his 300 Spartans who sacrificed themselves in an heroic defence so that the main army could retreat and re-group. Lord Byron swam across the Hellespont in 1807 though not, as far as is known, to keep a tryst with a lover. How surprising! It would have been in character. Alexander the Great also crossed but going the other way to Persia and Afghanistan where, no doubt, he was given as much trouble as were the British and Russians 2400 years later.

Of course, had Churchill pulled off Gallipoli, there would have been no "Lawrence of Arabia", and Lawrence would not have been buggered by a Turkish officer, nor would a thousand books have been written about him, nor would there have been a brilliant film featuring Peter O'Toole at his best made about him. There would also not have been a carve up of Mesopotamia and the Arabian Peninsula into petty kingdoms by the British. Imagine some Pro-Consul drawing lines in the sand, "This is for you Abdullah, call it Jordan. And this is yours Fouad. You can call it Saudi Arabia. As for what is left, Faisal, you can have the last bit and call it Iraq." Perhaps there would have been no war in Iraq, as I write, and the Americans would not be establishing the first colony of the Pax Americana. From camel drovers to Hashemite kings in one short war.

There were now three hours to fill before flying East to Ankara, Attaturk's modern capital, but this was too little time to explore the Emperor Constantine's capital, torn from Christendom by Mehmet the Conqueror in 1453. Thus beginning the 465 years of the Ottoman Empire that expanded to the gates of Vienna in 1529. The Turk didn't get in, or if he did not very far in. But he brought coffee, hence the Viennese coffeehouse and, I think, the crescent shaped croissant, though that somehow seemed to have leapfrogged to Paris.

Part of the time was required to keep appointments at the British Embassy and the American Embassy with their respective Trade Attachés, and the Turkish Chamber of Commerce. All three gave me valuable intelligence on matters of trade, the foundry industry in particular, and the disposition of industrial centres throughout the country.

The whole of Europe, East rather than West, plus the countries of the Levant, desperately needed capital investment. The West did not need it so much as it had largely overcome the need for external finance, meaning American, by about 1955, but not the other places which were very poor with little to export except some food and raw materials. It was easy to establish a requirement for capital plant; but the most difficult element in my job was to find out which countries had access to or offers of financial aid, particularly of a bi-lateral nature. E.g., perhaps the U.S.A. had agreed to give a loan of some millions of dollars to Turkey or Greece or the others, at a ridiculously low rate of interest provided the dollars were spent in the U.S.A. This was the vital information I sought from the Embassies visited. Strings attached to loans were thoroughly disliked. Many states wanted the money to spend as they wished, on huge white Mercedes and Swiss Bank Accounts (particularly in corrupt African states), or on building uneconomic steel plants and National Airlines. It puffed them up with pride and importance. If only those numerous and corrupt politicians, exploiters of their peoples had read that invocation in Ecclesiastes "Pride goeth before destruction and an haughty spirit before a fall". For many of them did indeed bite the dust in the fullness of time. Assassinated, bankrupted, exiled or otherwise disposed of.

None of my industrial visits were in or around Istanbul and with the half day left I chose to walk about, slowly because of the heat, looking at the people, sitting in cafés drinking Turkish coffee, supping an occasional glass of arak, looking at carpets and walking the Quay by the Galata Bridge which leads over to the Asian side of the town. I also met a very quirky and amusing Englishman, semi-domiciled in Istanbul in search of trade on behalf of a very grand British company. He proffered me a visiting card, supposedly belonging to a friend, which he said was good for a laugh when all else had failed.

The card owner might have been dyslexic, but I don't advise anybody to try and find this address in Istanbul.

The Blue Mosque and Hagia Sophia Basilica received scant attention and the Topkapi Palace Museum none at all, but twenty years later I came again with time to spend and it was well spent.

Now Ankara was a horse of quite another colour. Not a very apt metaphor perhaps for the capital of a country that had been dragged screaming out of the 19th century by a remarkable man. After all it had once been named Angora and had a thriving trade in the fine soft hair of Angora goats known as mohair. Attaturk hated Istanbul so much he never set foot in it between 1919 and 1927. To create a modern Turkey he knew he had to destroy the influence of the Sultan, the mosque and the veil. As far as he was concerned Istanbul could drop off the edge of Europe into the Bosphorus and take with it the pervasive, decadent influence in the Italian phrase "la dolce vita". So he built from scratch the ugly, aesthetically un-pleasant but practical and efficient new capital of Ankara. Everything was there, State Government, administration, law, architects, engineers, de-signers, men AND women of ideas. Those who are called today "movers and shakers". Mustafa Kemal Attaturk died tragically young, 58, in 1938 but in the short span of 19 years he laid a strong foundation for the future, too solid and strong to be destroyed by forces of re-action.

Ankara was the place to be if you wanted to know the route the Turks were taking towards raising the living standards generation, by a combi-nation of Western capitalism, tempered by the people's needs of human-ism and welfare. There was no room for the dirigiste socialist dialectics.

The Common Market, as the E.U. was then called, was in the process of making a loan of 175,000,000 dollars and private sources in the U.S.A. about 35,000,000 dollars. Already Chrysler and several tractor companies were building plants. Vitality and tremendous energy were busy building an industrial state. It was akin to the U.K. in the early 19th century, except that most of the basic ideas and inventions had to be imported. Islam, almost since Mohammed, had shown little interest in improving the material state of mankind. That was the business of Allah, if he so wished.

In six days I was in the plants of six potential customers with whom, in the fullness of time, I expected to be in negotiation. It did not take much digging to unearth the distasteful fact that palm greasing at high levels remained, though less apparent than in the days of the Sultan. You can no more take corruption out of the Levant than the Levant out of corruption. But, who are we to talk? The Western providers of armaments, chemical plants and high dams did not sell their products solely on quality. Ask any Saudi princeling about that. He will talk about it if you bribe him enough.

I was well pleased with my week in Turkey.

The Lebanon

Before pushing on from the land of the Sultans and Caliphs to the land of the Pharaohs it seemed a brilliant idea to spend a thoroughly idle weekend in the very centre of the Levant, the part which gave shape and meaning to the rest. Beirut was best because it had several flights daily to Cairo. From wealth to poverty in 300 miles. To understand the Lebanon one must take on board that it is tiny, only 150 miles long by 30 miles wide at its widest, and with a history stretching from 5,000BC until now (and still making history). And from at least 1,500BC it has been a civilised place of consequence. Throughout all that time its inhabitants must have been extraordinarily wise, energetic and adventurous. To be the creator of a school of law before the birth of Christ, and its earlier seafarers, the Phoenicians sailing to Cornwall, navigating by the stars to buy tin and, if you can believe Herodotus, sailing through the Pillars of Hercules South to the Cape of Good Hope. All the time increasing in wealth through a highly developed nose for trade allied to a liking for risk taking. Cedar to Solomon to build his temple in 750BC. Cedar and pine to Egypt, bringing back marble and papyri, which they exported throughout the Mediterranean. Clever middlemen, papyrus was called byblia – books – and hence the word "Bible".

What opulence was to be seen during my weekend visit to the Lebanon in July 1961! Grand hotels of the 19th century, St. Georges, wherein I stayed, the Bristol, the Phoenicia and the Vendôme, it was no wonder that for generations Beirut wore the sobriquet of "Paris of the East". There were such splendid restaurants and tearooms, such fashion – haute couture to rival Europe, such beautiful women, and such wickedness. Well, it must have been like that mustn't it? And then the Civil War of 1974 reduced two thirds of the city to rubble on the same scale of Berlin in World War II. Re-building has naturally been in the most modern of modern styles, so now, from the sea, it must look something like Chicago on Lake Michigan.

This is no ordinary people. Today's Levantine is very much like his ancestors. Wars come, wars go, there have been several serious earthquakes, destruction by Romans, Persians and Crusaders, but after every catastrophe he picked himself up, dusted himself down, picked up the pieces and put them together again.

How can it be that such a diversity of religions, Muslims (Sunni and Shi'ite), Druse (a mixture of Zoroastrianism, Islam and Gnosticism), Greek Orthodox and Maronite, and more political beliefs than you could shake a stick at could live side by side, though as mixed up as a fruit salad? Well, the answer to that is that they did, though the pot simmered always just below boiling point and, at well spaced intervals, boiled over with horrible, cruel consequences. This is as it has been, at least during the nearly 500 years of Turkish rule, themselves followers of Mohammed but not Arabs. The Koran as a choice from the sword was brought to the Levant 800 years before the Turks came. So, with Islam the dominant religion with the most followers, your average observer might think the Arab was top dog. By no means! The financial, commercial and intellectual affairs have been largely developed by the Christian minority and of this the Maronites in particular. Responsibility for this and the schism that was caused between Muslim and non-Muslim lay with the Turkish over-lords. Trade and finance had never been high on their priority list. Military and political control was of paramount importance. To be in a position of national or local authority one needs to be of the True Faith, no infidels need apply. So finance and trade, etc., became the pre-occu-pation of the non-Muslim, which the Turk seemed to welcome as the production of wealth pleased the Sultan back in Constantinople. In short, the non-Arab was good at education, the Arab was not clever in trade and the accumulation of wealth and did not seem to care. And that is what has caused the occasional explosion of community unrest since the departure of the Turk in 1917 and was the prime cause, along with the Jewish problem, of the 1974 Civil War. The pot is simmering at the moment and will undoubtedly boil over again soon.

There is a parallel with events in the U.K., though for different and quite benign reasons. On August 23rd 1572 20,000 Huguenots were mas-sacred in Paris on St. Bartholomew's Day, which gave its name to the mas-sacre. The Huguenots were Protestants and many of the survivors fled to England. The artisans among them created the English silk trade. Others became engineers, architects, bankers and lawyers. The country benefited enormously from this relatively small number of immigrants and the posi-tions they held in public life were out of all proportion to their numbers. If you look in a telephone directory and see a French name it is better than an even chance that ancestors of that name's owner were Huguenots.

Later in the last quarter of the 19th century, Jews fleeing the Pogroms of Poland and Russia arrived in England and they prospered for the same reasons that the Huguenots prospered, and the U.K. prospered mightily from their arrival too. Both of them practised the Protestant work ethic which created the wealth of the Anglo Saxon countries, notably in the U.S.A. They were, of course, the Levantines of the North.

Imagine walking through the narrow winding streets of Beirut, as chic as the Rue Royale, as confident, as opulent as Bond Street, but with the smells of the Orient and languorous sensual perfumes unknown in the West. It was another world with no apparent strife but a very French am-bience, for the Lebanon was mandated to France in 1918 and remained so until 1940. Whatever may be said about the French, nobody denies their sense of style. And wherever they are, for as little time as a generation, they leave their culture and language like no other nation. On the language side of things they need not have bothered for, to their intense anger, the whole world either speaks English or is learning to speak English. Our ultimate revenge.

The pace of commercial life in the ancient courtyards behind the massive wooden doors was doubtless frenetic, but in the avenues and faubourgs, in the Café de la Paix, Café de Sport and similar places, life was spent in a leisurely, laid back fashion. Backgammon pieces clicked, worry beads were caressed and the aroma of sweet tobacco filled the night air in competition with the jasmine. Men were seated or reclining smoking the nargileh, hubble bubble pipe to you and me, in which the tobacco smoke passes through water in a glass vessel before entering the mouth.

All that, my friends, in this year of Grace 2003AD is gone, or nearly gone and is the victim of war, civil war, religious intolerance, the helicopter gunship and the stand-off bomb which a pilot can deliver when miles from the target with no danger to himself.

The Levant attracted the adventurous of the English, particularly in the late 18th and 19th centuries. Numerous English ladies were attracted, particularly Lady Hester Stanhope who spent the last twenty years of her life near Sidon. She was the niece of William Pitt the Younger and social hostess to the unmarried Pitt at No. 10, Downing Street. After his death in 1806 and the death of her fiancée fighting with Wellington, she sailed to the Levant and never returned to England. She bought a monastery, not a difficult thing to do as they had escaped the vandalism of Henry the VIIIth, meddled in local politics, took a succession of Arab lovers and was generally thought to be mad by the natives though respected by them. Mad or not she was smart enough to prefer the Lebanon to Georgian London.

If you want to see Crusader Castles, palaces and churches of every period from pre-Christian synagogues to Byzantine Greek, and mosques with exquisitely beautiful shining domes and slender minarets: if you want azure sea, soft sandy beaches, with towering mountains as dramatic as Switzerland, then this tiny country, half the size of Wales, beckons the traveller, rather than the tourist.

On an eccentric note, while the Syrians pounded the Israelis with artillery over the narrow Bekaa Valley, which continued daily for many months, a vigneron was labouring in his vineyard in the Bekaa Valley underneath the shellfire. His name is Serge Hochar, and his vineyard is Chateau Muzor. During the whole period of the wars, both civil and uncivil, he never lost a harvest and made a red wine that can stand proudly in the presence of all but a handful of the great reds of Bordeaux in the Medoc. It was to my great regret that I did not make the effort to visit him in 1961. He is still there today and his wine is well known in the U.K. to those who know about such things.

Egypt

On the Sunday night I flew to Cairo.

I was first in Cairo in late 1940. It was then a city of one and a quarter to one and a half millions and, perhaps, could be described as Beirut writ large. In July 1961 the population was guessed to be at ten millions and in 1998, my last visit, you could choose a number off the top of your head and if it was in the region of sixteen millions it was probably as near as anybody was going to get to the correct figure, including the Egyptian Government.

No doubt about it, Cairo was a culture shock even then. Now it is a cultural nightmare. Hardened, old worldly wise cynic that I am, it is distasteful to see sheep being despatched with the knife on the roadside in the centre of a city even if it was Ramadan. My task in Egypt was the same as in Turkey but the approach had to be different. The Turks were reasonably organised, the Egyptians were not. The followers of Islam are not monolithic, they can be as different as a denizen of Betws-y-Coed is from a Wimbledon suburbanite. I don't know what it was, the burden of history, the diet of beans and pulses, the even tenor of the Nile which induces such somnolence in the men as to suggest the tobacco in their hubble bubble pipes is cut with "certain substances" as our police would say. But charm! They have it in bucketsful. Of the many people I have met, the Egyptian comes out well up in the charm league. The trouble is, leaving everything to God, "Inshallah" (God willing), is a b it delay making.

In the 1950's I regularly visited Ireland, the Republic not Ulster, which is another kettle of fish. There was not a lot going on and a framework for industry was moving slowly. Intelligent as are the Irish, much technical help was required and they looked to the Midlands, particularly in the Birmingham area, and many engineers went over to places such as Waterford, Wexford, Limerick and Cork. These were men who, in Birmingham or Coventry, worked a very long day, took little time off for lunch, and were bastards for discipline and left late in the evening. But in Ireland they quickly changed to a late start, 3 pints of Guinness with lunch and an early finish. It took your average Brummy about a month to go native in Ireland. There was something Irish about the Egyptians. Could they have [picked up a way of life from the Irish soldiers who, as part of the British Army, were in Egypt from about 1870 to 1956? For most of that time, especially in the 19th century, 50% of the private soldiers were Catholic Irish and 50% of the officers Anglo Irish Protestants.

I began to feel a bit helpless in the face of such innocent resistance to the Protestant work ethic and the feeling of "Oh! Sod it! What the Hell!" crossed my mind from time to time. And another thing, the 30 or so words of Arabic picked up as a soldier 20 years earlier came out as though I were a Pentecostal "speaking in tongues". The Egyptians were highly amused. Nevertheless I was there to work, so with no useful assistance from the British Embassy, the American Embassy, or the Egyptian statutory bodies (Chambers of Commerce, etc.), I hired a car and started to 'cold call' on the small list of foundries whose names I had obtained in England from various sources. This took me into the Nile Delta, south of Cairo into such hellholes as Zagaziq (famous for its mosquitoes), El Wasta and Ismailia on the Suez Canal. There is an unusual pot pourri of odours you will rarely find anywhere else on earth, consisting, as far as I could define it, of dog shit, camel shit, human and goat. Teeming with humanity, they lived as close together as bees in a hive. Later, back in Cairo and speaking to Cairenes, they were full of admiration, indeed awe, on hearing where I had been. They were places to which they had never been and to which they would never go, and yet, in the foundries on which I called, the reception was like that given to the prodigal son by his father. Had there been fatted calves they would have been butchered in my honour. In no time at all, cigarettes, fresh lime juice and arak were on the table. Oh, and tap water which in those days I drank safely. The Mullahs of Saudi and Iran were never best pleased with the louche Egyptian attitude to alcohol which was "Oh, what the Hell".

As to the foundries they were not exactly working at the pit face of technology. It was like watching a film in slow motion. Of the foundries on my list all would have been closed down in Western Europe, or Eastern for that matter. There were just two for whom the Government has screwed money out of the World Bank, generally regarded as the milch cow for the Third World. Equipment had been purchased but it was the wrong equipment. New plant needs a new infrastructure of buildings and engineering, otherwise it is like putting new wine into old bottles. Egypt was not short of quite bright graduates, trained abroad. But that is never the answer without the rest of the expenditure. Tens of thousands of graduates spew forth from Egyptian Universities every year. Few want to dirty their hands in industry (come to think of it that's how it is in the U.K. at the moment). There is vast unemployment and a new Egyptian is born every forty seconds. What they really want to be is unemployed doctors, unemployed lawyers and unemployed dentists. And very good at it they are too.

When one thinks of the engineering genius and technical craft that 4,000 years earlier had built the Pyramids of Ghisa and the Temples of Luxor and Aswan, one wonders what happened in between then and now. They are virtually the same people. There were no Diaspora or pogroms to disperse them all over the world, as happened to the Jews. There was little or no movement of people, if only because the natural fertility of the land watered by the Nile had never failed to feed them.

But my time was not wasted. There was much to see again from my youth of twenty years earlier. As in the Lebanon the French influence was out of all proportion to the handful of years they were in Egypt as conquerors. A mere three or four with Napoleon until Nelson did the business in Aboukir Bay and drove them back to France. Trade and commerce brought them again and the middle classes, especially in Alex, were more likely to speak French than English, while French culture in the form of books, plays and music was much admired. Now English, force majeur, is the lingua franca.

After Nasser, in fact before his early death, Cairo started to fall apart, and as much evidence as possible of the 80 years of British occupation was removed. It was the re-writing of history. Familiar Street names were changed. Sharia Suleiman Pasha became Tabris Street, Sharia Emadel Dine became Ramses Street, and the English Cathedral was pulled down. The great monuments of the middle ages remained, such as Saladin's Citadel and the University of Al Azhar. Also, and surprisingly, the Christian Coptic centre remained as a complete way of life, with dwellings, churches, shops, schools of the Coptic people, Christians since the 2nd century AD, and in Cairo and Alexandria anyway. Living peacefully with the Muslims. Frequently they also reach high office in State or Provincial Governments. Nasser was a sort of New Labour "De son jour" and just as full of spindoctory bullshit.

Above all things I wanted to visit the Gezira Club. It is on the island of Gezira in the middle of the Nile, across the 6th October Bridge (formerly Kasrel Nil Bridge) and is an outrageous anachronism, the GeziraRacing and Sporting Club. Built by the cavalry of the British Army in the 19th century, who seemed to be on permanent posting to Egypt, it gave them all the comforts and much more luxury than they ever had in London. It consisted of a racecourse, polo field, cricket ground, numerous croquet lawns, swimming pool, restaurants and accommodation, with a membership of about 400. In wartime, after a long spell in the desert, the common soldiery was allowed to use the Club whilst on leave in Cairo. It had been a lifesaver and I dearly wanted to see it again. So I went. There was a milling crowd trying to force an entrance but an efficient police force, used to that sort of thing, beat them severely about the body with clubs. When they saw me, and I could not have looked less Egyptian, they waved me through with a smile. The place was a mess. No money had been spent on it for years and, I was told, the membership was now 30,000. Unexpectedly the croquet lawn was still in use and I sat watching a game flanked by some very old Greeks who had survived Nasser's expulsion of the Brits in 1956. We talked a lot of the Cairo of long ago and, to their delight, I gave them a fairly recent copy of The Times which I had bought in Beirut. They say you should never go back.

I left Cairo the same day, not even bothering to visit the Pyramids, which by then were almost a part of Cairo suburbia. My hotel, as in the days of long ago, sent a porter to the Central Station to buy my rail ticket, thus sheltering me from the huge crowds which always seem to fill the stations in poor countries.

A lovely train, air conditioned, did the 110 mile journey to Alex in two hours. I was booked into the Cecil Hotel on the Corniche, a little tatty but hardly changed since I last saw it in 1942, but famous for its use in the Alexandria Quartet novels of Lawrence Durrell, and the TV series of Olivia Mannings Balkan Trilogy novels. It positively oozed with ghostly atmosphere and was much used by Greek and other elderly émigrés. They welcomed a fresh European visitor and were eager to talk. I am very fond of run down, but very comfortable, hotels.

Alexandria is as different from Cairo as Venice is from Rome, and the people are not Arab in the way of Cairenes. The mixture pre-dates Cleopatra, with Greeks, Cretans, Lebanese and Syrians. They were Christians almost as early as the Copts and it was thought surprising that, when offered the Koran or a sword after a short siege by a Saracen army from Syria they chose the Koran. As a punishment the greatest and most famous library in Christendom was destroyed.

Amron, the victorious general, first sought the advice of the Caliph Omar in Damascus before engaging in such an act of vandalism. Omar replied "If these writings of the Greeks agree with the book of God they are useless and need not be preserved. If they disagree they are pernicious and ought to be destroyed." So they were used to fuel the public baths which had been built by the Romans.

Cairo is a city of the East, Alexandria of the Mediterranean, popular with the Greeks for two millennia, and with the French. Any lover of Laurence Durrell's novels would revel in it, dump as it is compared with the 20's and 30's when he was there. Old Greek cotton dealers on the Cotton Exchange are there in a few handfuls, but you need to search hard for signs of the beautiful and decadent town it had been since the French fin de siècle.

There was no immediate business and not much, I thought, for the future so I departed, returning to Cairo to catch my early flight the next day to Athens, en route to Israel. Alas! The train was missed and my fault, too complicated to explain. In desperation I became the fourth passenger in a taxi so battered its provenance was a mystery. The price was alarmingly low but the driver promised to deliver me to my hotel that day. It became a hilarious trip through the densely crowded Delta towns and villages. The desert road would have been quicker and nicer but there was no choice. After ten miles the engine boiled, the driver stopped, lifted up the bonnet and replaced the broken fan belt with a spare, which he happened to have, and we were off in no more than five minutes. In Egypt only a fool drives without a spare fan belt.

How I blessed those thirty words of Arabic, and how delighted my fellow passengers were to hear them. We stopped twice for coffee and other refreshment, and there was no question of these poor people letting the rich one pay. The journey passed quickly enough and by no means in silence. These kind people went miles out of their way to drop me off at my hotel in the centre of Cairo. I had half a bottle of scotch in my kit which I offered the driver. He didn't refuse it. For those who might be interested in Cairo I recommend the novels of Naguib Mahfouz. He is very old and wrote about life in Cairo since about 1930. Well written, fascinating and gripping you will find them in most libraries.

I was in Athens at nine o'clock next morning and in Tel Aviv by midday, only 200 miles away from Cairo as the crow flies.

Israel

People intent on going to Israel for the first time, and hardly anybody goes without the burden of anti-Semitism to some degree, would benefit from reading a little history of how the Jews finally ended up where they started from in the country they left 2,000 years earlier. And all that time they remained a single united people in whichever country reluctantly allowed them to stay, held together by a universal hatred and the strongest of religious faiths, rivalled only by that of their bitterest enemy and, ironically, brother Semite, the Arab.

One should reflect on the fact that a nation of 6 millions (in 1948 only about 1 million) is surrounded on every side, except by the sea, by some 200 million followers of Islam who, at best, want you dead or, at worst, driven into the sea or to somewhere else. With this knowledge, as Dr.Johnson said of the man who was to be hanged in two week's time, "the mind becomes greatly concentrated". Then, having defeated your mortal enemy in 1948, 1956, 1967 and 1973, (forget the stories that without American money it could not have been done, it is always the man behind the gun rather than the gun in front of the man that wins.)you spend the next fifty years awaiting the next Arab War, whilst at the same time building a nation from scratch. Take all that on board and the Israeli people can be judged rather more objectively.

So I arrived in Tel Aviv in the heat of a Middle Eastern Summer, which was tempered by the pleasant zephyrs coming off the Mediterranean but a few yards from the line of hotels in Ha-Yarkon Street. One of these is the Dan Hotel to which I will refer later. Tel Aviv had the feeling of a modern, but somewhat jerrybuilt European town, and no feeling at all of the Orient, of Araby, or the "Mysterious East". But first there was the reception by immigration which was not very nice, in fact, distinctively unfriendly towards foreigners, at least compared with the lackadaisical ways normal at that time in airports of the West, where people in the 1960's were unaccustomed to fighting for their lives. The Israelis have not remained free from highjacking and bomb outrages by being either nice to either arrivals OR departures. The best words to describe the long interrogation should be 'severe' and 'thorough', "Where are you from?" "For what purpose have you come?" "Do you know anybody in Israel?" "What is in your luggage?" "Let's have a look!" "Have you been here before?" "Where will you be staying?" "How long will you be staying?" and so on for 30 minutes or so. It was very annoying and could induce anger. But it was not personal, and on thinking about it, very necessary. Lone travellers and one's with thick passports full of visas seemed to attract quite outstanding interest.

My hotel was in Tel Aviv because it is the commercial centre, and secular, while Jerusalem disdains trade and is severely religious. In Jerusalem the Sabbath is harshly kept but in Tel Aviv it is obeyed in the breach rather than in the spirit. Also the industrial base is in the Northern towns of Tel Aviv, Haifa, Netanya and quite a few of the kibbutz settlements. This tiny country, in the field of engineering and foundry practice, provided more potential business than Greece and Egypt put together. They made tanks of high quality, importing only the engines, had a flourishing arms industry and nuclear weapons, to which they will not willingly admit, of course. But they are permanently in danger and one day their nuclear option may need to be used, or at least threatened. Armaments apart their foundries and engineering plants have the primary aim of making Israel as near self sufficient as possible. Their second aim is to build up an export trade. Already they were a net exporter of fruit and some foods, which was grown by intensive irrigation, making the desert bloom and growing two blades of grass where hitherto there had been only one. In the field of irrigation they are among the world leaders and scientists who were paid very little did much of the research on a kibbutz.

There was a tremendous reservoir of intellect, which was a veritable powerhouse in Israel. Those who survived the Holocaust, and their children who made it to the haven of Israel were, or became, writers, musicians, engineers, physicists, chemists, architects, philosophers, lawyers (whom they could have done without), doctors, surgeons, etc. With this stock of brains, anything and everything became possible. In successive taxi rides the drivers were, respectively, a violinist from the pre-War Berlin Philharmonic Orchestra and a lecturer in history from Hanover University. They were not yet in suitable work, but they were happy. Few doubt that the murder of Jews in the gas chambers, and the departure of survivors to other lands so impoverished the intellectual base of Germany that it has not, even today, recovered from that loss.

I was only in Israel for seven days, which was not long enough, but sufficient to identify it as the most important centre of industrial development in the Levant. In the fullness of time they might even become a prime supplier to the enemies at the gate. Stranger things have happened.

The Dan Hotel was not just an hotel, but an hotel with air conditioning, one of the few in Tel Aviv. So in the suffocating night heat I spent a fair time there, in the bar. Then the tricks that memory plays brought something to the top of the pile. I said to the barman "Does Sydney Stanley ever come here?" "Yes." He said. He knew at once whom I was asking about. Now here is a fine tale to end a chapter.

In 1948 there was a scandal that shook the political world of the U.K. and nearly broke the Labour Government. A certain Sydney Stanley, con. artist, trader and fantasist, was accused of seeking to influence government departments b y bribery, the bestowal of gifts and flattery in order to obtain export and import licenses. Harold Wilson, President of the Board of Trade, instructed by the Prime Minister Clement Attlee, set up a Tribunal presided over by Mr. Justice Lynsky, to examine people, the papers and the facts. It was the lurid and often comic public proceedings of this Tribunal that led to the resignations of Mr. John Belcher, Parliamentary Secretary at the Board of Trade, for receiving small (very small) gifts. Poor innocent devil, formerly a railway clerk, promoted beyond his ability. It destroyed him, and also several other officials. One, I remember, was Secretary of the Labour Trades Union Congress. Stanley had spread his net wide and others were smeared, Dalton, Cripps and Bevin each suffered moments of indignity at the Tribunal.

Stanley was brought to trial at the Old Bailey and prosecuted by the Attorney General, Sir Hartley Shawcross, famous at Labour's triumph after the election victory of 1945 for shouting "We are the masters now!", a statement which proved a great hostage to fortune in the future. There then followed days of cut and thrust humour, worthy of the Palladium, as Stanley was examined by Sir Hartley. The case was cut and dried but Stanley had been granted bail, so before the judge could sum up he jumped bail and fled to Israel with whom the U.K. had no extradition treaty, and, strangely enough, as I write, it still does not.

The next night I met Sydney. He looked very old, very unkempt and rather sad, wishing, he said, he were back in London. Strange that, most of the villains on the run in Spain say they miss London. He was quite talkative after I plied him with whisky and why not, I was speaking to a man who had held the world's stage in London for months during l948. Stanley mere proved "the larceny in the soul". He was a willing buyer and they were willing sellers.

Two days later I was home. I remember it was raining, and cold.

THE USA PART 2 (VALETE)

THE SECRET OF SUCCESS IS HONESTY AND FAIR DEALING.

IF YOU CAN FAKE BOTH OF THESE YOU'VE GOT IT MADE

Sometime in September 1963 I was seated in a plane en route from Milan to Heath Row. It was a Friday afternoon, and I had been making the same flight, on the same day, for six weeks. Each Sunday night I would return to Milan to continue a task that was troublesome and fraught with an irritating mixture of success and failure, in one of Fiat's automotive foundries in Turin, bearing the idyllic name Fonderia Mirofiore. It was to continue for several more weeks. Opposite, that is across the gangway, sat an elderly bloke. I was reading the day's copy of the Corriere della Sera in the absence of an English paper, and was not in a conversational mood. He leant over, touched my arm, and said "What do you think about this?" He held a watch in his hand and passed it over for me to read an inscription on the back. Now I must dig deep into my memory, but it said something like this "Presented to James M. Swartz by 419 Post of the U.S. Marine Corps to commemorate his presentation of a Scroll of Honorary Corps Membership to Winston S. Churchill – May 7th 1947". "Interesting" I said and continued reading. A few minutes later he jogged my arm again and asked what I thought about Churchill. The last thing I wanted to do at that moment was to talk, and despite my admiration of Churchill as soldier, orator, statesman, and as one of the greatest men who had ever lived, I got quite pissed off and gave this American a good dose of Devil's Advocacy. I pulled Churchill apart, told of his sending troops to break the Welsh miners' strike at Tonypandy, his dangerous, ill planned Gallipoli campaign, his changing of party in the House of Commons (not once but twice). This amused Swartz no end for he was the recipient of the watch and he said he wanted to continue the talk. You'll hardly credit this but he had two ladies with him and he persuaded one of them to take my seat, while I moved over to sit between him and the other, who was Mrs. Lora Swartz. He had to persuade me also, of course, but my resistance had flagged – it is as well to know when you are beaten. The story was that four of them had set off from Baltimore, Maryland, on a round the world trip. The absent one was Victor Frankel, husband of the lady now in my seat, chickened out at San Francisco and went home to his business. So Swartz was now lumbered with two women, one of whom, Mrs. Frankel, decided she preferred Bali to Baltimore. So for the remaining hour of the flight we talked about many things, not only about Churchill's life, about which he was remarkably well informed, but politics, business and matters of philosophical nature. Jimmy Swartz was a cultivated, shrewd man. Only months later did I realise that he was subtly submitting me to a viva voce, but for what? I mellowed somewhat under his charm and told him stories about Churchill which he had never heard before. Like his encounter in the House of Commons with the Liverpool M.P. Bessie Braddock "Winston", she said, "You are drunk!" "True", he replied, "And you are ugly, but tomorrow I will be sober." And there was Churchill's joke about Clement Atlee. Atlee arrived at the Parliament in a taxi, the door opened, then shut but nobody got out.

We arrived at London on time, shook hands all round and went our separate ways. That is the end of that, I thought. But it wasn't, not by a long chalk.

Work for the remainder of the year was much the same as for the previous nine months. I was in and out of France, Germany and Italy with one important foray into Jugoslavia. It also saw the assassination of Jack Kennedy in Dallas on November 22nd, which shook the world to its foundations. The world's media, as always, recovered quickly, wiped its eyes, ceased the crocodile tears and got on with the serious business of conspiring, theorising, character destruction and, most important, Jack's bedtime romps with Marilyn Monroe. This was later finessed into romps à trois, the third member of the trio being his brother, Bobby, also to be assassinated on 6th June 1968.

My affairs, however, were about to change dramatically. After a working life containing more time absent from home, that even then was considered abnormal, and for nearly ten years, I decided to, as it were, cross the Rubicon and leave my American employers. It was a nightmare decision for I had been happy in my job. Family pressures, though growing, had not yet reached dangerous levels, and my American boss certainly did not want me to leave. It is laughable when, in recent years, politicians have given the weasel worded excuse for quitting the rat race of Parliament and Whitehall as wanting to spend more time with their family: this from people at home most nights, or at least every weekend. The expression "at home with my family" has become a newspaper jibe, but six to eight months a year abroad, 50,000 miles of driving and another 20,000 of flying was a different kettle of fish.

Because of my intense European travel and contacts, British compa-nies from time to time made overtures to me, suggesting I might care to work for them. When I spelt out the nature of my work, and the immense difficulties involved in international selling, they were aghast. In that period, exports from the U.K. were usually to the soft, complacent countries of the Commonwealth and Empire. Certainly not to Germans speaking German, the French speaking French, or the Italians speaking Italian. They thought it should have involved an airtrip or two, handing over a few leaflets (in English), then perhaps a good lunch before picking up a good order. When I told them it might mean a client holding on to your own or technician's passports until the project was in and working, this, of course, only in the Iron Curtain countries, and the amount of my present salary, they quickly lost interest. They were not accustomed to a salesman in receipt of a salary, which exceeded that of a Chief Executive. I was amused but not surprised by their re-actions. They would never have tolerated, as did my patient and farseeing Americans a wait of two years before I obtained my first substantial order from Jugoslavia.

With my wife's full support the decision was made to leave my Amer-icans and start a new job in January 1964. It would be to some intent in competition with them but they were not concerned. My boss even sug-gested emigration to Cleveland as his Personal Assistant. My wife advised against it on the grounds of my being temperamentally unsuited to being turned into an American. I had no difficulty in agreeing with her. So, in partnership with a middling sized English company whose equipment was compatible with my engineering experiences, I set up a foundry equipment division. That act of job change involved a voluntary acceptance of a 60% salary reduction in spite of having two sons in private education, a largish house and corresponding mortgage. In retrospect it didn't seem to matter a damn and my wife was even less worried than I was.

My new company was in Bognor, a modest 37 miles daily car journey. But I began to hate the place and started to re-act to it as did George V, whose last words on his death bed on being told he would soon be well enough to visit Bognor , and are probably apocryphal, said "Bugger Bognor". For years after I could never remember the place I drove to nearly every day for eight months. My partner and I were intellectually philosophically miles apart on how a business should function. So we parted, amicably enough, for me to do as I should have in the beginning, set up my own business. Some people are good in a team, others are not. As with Lord Beaverbrook, owner of Express Newspapers and wartime Cabinet Minister, I believe that a committee should consist of three people, two of whom are permanently absent. I expected to take five years to regain my 1963 income; it was done in three.

I have digressed rather. In the December of 1963, my last month of employment with my Americans, and always while I was absent abroad, there were several phone calls for me at home. They were always in the early hours between 2 and 4am. My wife did not think this at all funny. The messages were garbled, indistinct and probably from the U.S.A., the sender being unaware of time differences. Finally contact was made at a more friendly hour when I was back home. The caller was Jimmy Swartz, and he wanted to talk about Frankel who had legged it back to his company from San Francisco having set off from Baltimore with Jimmy and their respective wives on a world tour. Briefly, he had "sold" me to Frankel as a possible Personal Assistant, and Frankel wanted to talk. I told Jimmy that I was committed to a new job in the U.K. and there was a moral agreement, which I was not inclined to break. Anyway, I suggested that Frankel should write to me. This he did, explaining his business. He was a civil engineer on a large scale. Anyone who knows the geography of the U.S.A. will know Chesapeake Bay on the Atlantic coast, sometimes known as the Chesapeake Roads, which lead several hundred miles to

Washington where it becomes the Potomac River. It is a wide expanse of salt water and was the route taken by the British in the War of 1812 on the way to burning down the White House. At a narrow place not far from Washington, Frankel's company built a road tunnel under the Chesapeake 20 miles long. It was a feat in the same league as the Channel Tunnel but 40 years earlier. That was the sort of firm for whom Swartz wanted me to work. As luck would have it I intended in May 1964 to attend an International Exhibition in Detroit, and told Jimmy we could meet in Baltimore and talk with Frankel. I was deeply flattered. Who would not be?

In May I took my sixth trip to America. It was my last business trip but quite a few were to be made in subsequent years up to AD2000. The Swartz – Frankel was best done first so I flew into Washington to be met by Swartz and taken the 30 miles to Baltimore. There, to my delight, we boarded a helicopter, property of Baltimore Contractors Inc., along with a director of the firm, which was wholly owned by Frankel. We flew to three sites on which, respectively, were being built a shopping mall, an industrial complex and an office block. These were in different parts of Maryland and Virginia with about 30 minutes flying time in between. This, I supposed, was a display of Frankel power and influence in civil engineering circles. If I was expected to be impressed, then I was, deeply.

Back in Baltimore Jimmy dropped me off in a stylish motel, which he happened to own, and arranged to have me collected next morning. It had been quite a day but nothing compared with what was to follow. A man in his 40's collected me and we drove to a shop in downtown Baltimore, a large fur emporium, to have called it a shop or boutique would have been too modest. This was Jimmy's major business; he imported and sold furs in an age when a lady could wear mink without paint being thrown over her. The man who collected me from the motel turned out to be a murderer, on parole from the State Pen., working for Jimmy. The jigsaw pieces that, when complete, would show a picture of Jimmy Swartz were gradually taking shape. But the vital parts were yet to be slotted in.

It was a balmy day, no wind, about 70°F and sunny. American seasons are not as defined as ours. In the Mid-West, St. Louis for example,

Monday in April can have a temperature of 20°F and Wednesday 70°F. virtually no Spring. Maryland is a bit like that. "Let's go for a walk", said Jimmy, "I'll show you something of Baltimore". It is not a small town, with perhaps 200,000 inhabitants, but the State Capital of Maryland, the smallest, except for Delaware, of the thirteen States who signed the Declaration of Independence in 1776. As Benjamin Franklin said at the signing, "Either we hang together or we hang separately". The second Lord Baltimore was the first Governor of Maryland in 1634. It is also a substantial port on Chesapeake Bay. So we sauntered along, Jimmy being greeted on all sides "Morning Jimmy, how ya doin'?" by the locals, shop owners and others. He examined goods in this shop, picked up and bit an apple in another. Jimmy was what they call in the South, "A good ole boy".

Later we went to his home which was a non-working farm of about 50 acres on the outskirts of the city, a neo-colonial house but not anti-bellum, about 1860 and typical of the sort favoured by the slave owners of Virginia, Maryland and other Southern States. The exterior was old but the interior very modern and comfortable. There was a fair sized kidney shaped pool, very new, in fact, just completed said Jimmy by three men who had come from about 100 miles away bringing every device available of a mechanical nature, including a gun for spraying concrete. They did the job in four days. Very American. No wonder that in wartime they were building a 10,000 ton Liberty cargo ship every week.

Jimmy said he was so pleased with their work he was having a gold inscribed medal struck for each of them – also a very American thing to do. By contrast, and done by a very good local firm, I had a similar sized pool built in 1978, but it took four men four weeks or more to do it. How very English. It was not Jimmy's style to signal what he had in store for one. During lunch he asked if I would like to go on a sponsored walk which had been organised in a nearby park, nothing strenuous, more a gentle 3 mile stroll really, in aid of one of his pet charities. Well, a couple of girl bazooka bands, jugglers and fire eaters turned up and many. There were rather more than you would get at a vicar's tea party. Mrs. Swartz presided at lunch, a cultured, charming woman and, not uncommon among the ruling class in America, of a literary bent. She had had a romantic novel published in 1961 and she signed a copy before she gave it to me. Now, romantic novels are not my cup of tea. At home once more I read it, and I must say it was not like a Jeffrey Archer, the sort of book that once put down you can't pick it up again. She had a gift for narrative and dialogue that completely escaped the likes of Barbara Cartland. It also taught me how difficult novel writing is and why I should never try it. She wrote under the name of Anne Maturin, Lara Swartz being unsuitable for a novel entitled "A Dawn Set Free". But it was favourably reviewed in the newspapers of Baltimore and Washington.

The walk was not long, perhaps 3 miles, though for a people with their backsides almost welded to a car seat it was long enough. About one thousand people heeled and toed it and they looked quite different from an American crowd today. Few were noticeably fat and there were no massive 15 stone 12 year old hunks of junk food which in most parts of the U.S.A. today is the norm.

The day was a Saturday and Jimmy said he was going to take me to a public dinner where I would meet Vic. Frankel and some other interesting people. That was an understatement. The dinner took place in the Emerson Hotel, and bore the title "The Jefferson – Jackson Day Dinner, thrown by the Maryland Democratic Party every year. Thomas Jefferson, as everybody knows, or should know, was the third President of the U.S.A. and Andrew

Jackson the seventh. Heroes of the Democratic Party their names were often used to head up fund raising dinners.

Another part of the Swartz jigsaw puzzle had clicked into place, Jimmy was a Democratic activist. At the hotel he said he had something to attend to and handed me over to one William O'Brien, Treasurer of the State of Maryland, a tall red haired Irishman, with whom I felt comfortable. In the huge lobby I saw a man sprawled on a sofa with a short queue of men in a line waiting to speak to him. O'Brien took me to the head of the queue and introduced me to the man who seemed more comatose than awake. We talked briefly and moved away. I looked again at the men waiting to speak with Frankel. They held their hats in their hands and their heads were bowed like supplicants. At the time I sought for a word to describe them and came up with "humble", it was perfect. To

O'Brien I put the question, "Who are those men?" He replied somewhat hesitantly and I felt he had rather I had not asked, "Oh they are U.S. Congressmen, friends of Vic's, business friends". But there was one, standing slightly apart, with a familiar face, and I asked his name, "Spiro Agnew" replied O'Brien, "a very liberal Republican who is marked out for political advancement. But here he was, waiting in line to speak to the owner of one of the largest civil engineering groups in Virginia in an industry shot through with corrupt practice. It looked like a scene from "The Godfather" film with Frankel playing Marlon Brando's part.

In 1966 Agnew became Governor of Maryland and in 1968 Richard Nixon's vice presidential running mate. In 1973 he resigned for reasons never fully explained but believed to be of a financial nature. Much later I read a piece in The Guardian written by Adam Rafael, Washington correspondent, dated 1971, which told it all. There had been a huge row in Congress started by Mr. Hale Boggs, the House Majority Leader, about FBI phone tapping of Congressmen's telephone lines, including his. Boggs had become an object of investigation on the instructions of the Department of Justice into whether "Mr. Victor Frankel, a Baltimore civil engineering contractor, had sought to bring pressure to bear on Members of Congress to have construction claims settled favourably". A Grand Jury found that Mr.Frankel's company, Baltimore Contractors Inc., performed work on Mr. Boggs' Maryland home at a laughably low price to curry favour. This, of course, Congressman Boggs denied. The U.S. Attorney General, John Mitchell, refused to allow the Grand Jury to issue indictments. Mr. Mitchell, along with his boss Richard Nixon, was in serious trouble over the Watergate scandal and forced to resign in 1976.

More was to come, interesting people indeed! Jimmy, you didn't tell me the half of it. O'Brien and I were the last to enter the banqueting room, where about 500 people were seated at round tables of about a dozen guests. But there was a top long table of about twenty of the great and the good were seated. As we entered the room all faces seemed to turn in our direction. Don't ask me why. Clearly I was a stranger. Perhaps it was my un-American suit, my blue and white striped shirt in a sea of pure white shirts, or my longish English hair where short or crew cut hair was the fashion. At all events, close interest was shown, and even closer when O'Brien lead me up to the top table and placed me next to another familiar face, that of Senator Frank Church, Chairman of the Congressional Foreign Affairs Committee and internationally well known. Jimmy Swartz certainly had influence, and my always sensitive antennae were sending a frisson of something or other through my head.

This was a fund raising dinner in the big league on behalf of Senator Daniel B. Brewster, the Democratic candidate for the State Governorship in November 1964. He failed to make it, as I subsequently heard, and as far as I know was quite free of any taint of financial how's your father. Perhaps that is why he failed. It was of the genre known as a rubber chicken dinner, which reflected the nature of the food and it was also a booze free zone. About 500 people were seated and, it was whispered, the going rate was one thousand dollars a plate. The personal wealth represented would have excited Croesus. There were several minor Kennedys present, and a large bevy of Senators and Congressmen. Frank Church was a delightful, cultivated and witty man. Only in his 40's he was to die tragically two years later.

There was a postscript. Next day I received three telephone calls before ten o'clock, two from people who had been at the dinner and one from the local press. All had seen me arrive and, more importantly, where I had sat. Americans are very tribal, suspicious of outsiders and anxious to know who, what and where. They didn't find me a satisfactory source as I only said I was a friend of Jimmy Swartz.

Sunday was relatively quiet. Jimmy came round at a civilised hour and said he had a visit to make. We drove to the oldest part of Baltimore, full of three storied elegant houses dating from the early nineteenth century, but slightly run down. We parked outside one of them and Jimmy knocked but nobody came. The door was ajar so he pushed it open and yelled "Jack, are you there?" A voice replied, "Is that you, Jimmy? I've been expecting you, come right on up." Which we did, to the top, where an open door showed a large well appointed bedroom, a king sized bed supporting a large, overweight, unshaven man clad only in a vest and underpants. This was Jack Pollack. The conversation that followed was very informal, and the subject difficult to follow but, in essence, Jack, a long time supporter and contributor to the Democrats was in bad odour with some extremely important and influential Baltimore citizens and wanted to know if Jimmy could help him to get back in the swim, as it were. "What about a hundred thousand?" said Jimmy. "Are you sure that's enough?" said Jack. "Sure, I'm sure." Said Jimmy. And that ended the visit. Jack was put at ease and Jimmy had a cast iron guarantee of one hundred thousand dollars for party funds. What a fund raiser!

The day was not yet over. An incident was already in place to ambush me of a nature that, even in my wildest dreams, or should I say "wildest nightmares", I could never have imagined. In late afternoon Jimmy casually remarked "Did I ever tell you I am a prison visitor?" "No." I said, "You didn't." "Well, this evening my friend Joe Klein is coming with me to address the prisoners' Social Awareness Class at Maryland State Penitentiary, I don't know on what subject but would you like to come along?" "Why not?" I said, "I have never been inside a prison." So that was the evening fixed and at about six o'clock he picked me up. The prison was not far from the city centre, and when we were about ten minutes from it Jimmy said to me "Arthur, would you like to do me a big favour?" "Sure, Jimmy, if I can." "Arthur, I'm in a terrible fix, Joe Klein rang me about an hour ago to say he couldn't make it, and I've been unable to find a substitute speaker at such short notice. At that point my blood ran cold. I knew what was coming. "No! Jimmy," I shouted, "I won't do it!" "Come on, Arthur" he said, "With your international experience it'll be a piece of piss." More like a bucket of shit to be poured on me, I thought. "O.K. Jimmy" I said, "You've got me over a barrel. I'll do it."

In a couple of minutes we drew up outside a massive old Victoria jail, the Maryland State Penitentiary. It could have been Pentonville. I felt like a penitent all right, but for no reason. Dr. Johnson is supposed to have said that when a man is to be hanged in two weeks it concentrates his mind mightily. I was concentrating, and, with the luck that can help somebody not unaccustomed to being in tight spots, I had a brilliant idea. Here were men locked up for most of the rest of their natural lives, I would talk to them about another sort of prison. One with invisible walls, or almost invisible, the prison states of the U.S.S.R., East Germany, Czechoslovakia, Hungary, etc, in which over the previous eight years I had spent quite a lot of time. This, remember, was 1964. What a relief, I'd cracked it, and was already filling with the confidence of the experienced con. man, which I hoped I was not.

We drove through the massive gates to be met by the Assistant Governor who led us literally behind bars into an assembly area. It was crowded with men in white shirts and a lot of warders, or prison officers as we are supposed to call them these days. It was not easy to tell prisoners from warders, and clearly black was the flavour of the month. We got into an ancient, wheezing lift, which gasped and puffed its way up to the Assistant Governor's office. A young black operated the lift and he was cheerful and disposed to chat. So I asked him how old he was and how long he had been inside. Twenty five, he said, and since he was fifteen. With luck he might be paroled in five years. He had a knife scar from one eye down to his chin. "Done inside?" I asked. "You bet." He replied.

In his office the Assistant Governor explained the position. About one hundred lifers, all murderers, formed the Social Awareness Class. At least all were sentence for murder, the rules of evidence in the American South being somewhat lax compared to the U.K. The trials could be something of a lottery, especially when the accused was black. Once a month they were treated to a talk from somebody outside of the person service, and it had become the great event of the month. The Assistant Governor said it played an important part in keeping up their morale. They would expect a talk of about forty minutes, followed by questions and answers. So we went into the lecture room to be met by a sea of black faces dappled here and there by the occasional white. I didn't announce the subject, just moved into the events of the last eight years, which I had experienced in those countries behind the Iron Curtain, as Churchill had named it. They remained quite silent for the first ten minutes, trying to fathom out my accent. I doubt any of them had ever previously heard an English voice. Then they loosened up, moving in their seats, egging me on, wanting more and excited about the subject. So I told them about life in Czechoslovakia, Hungary, East Germany and Poland and the hundreds of political executions from 1948 to the present day, the food shortages that kept everybody on short rations. Where once or twice a year you might see oranges in the shops but not bananas, apples but not pears, black shoes in the shops but not brown. I told of constant queues outside shops when a rumour spread like wild fire that something was about to appear on sale. Everybody walked about carrying a bag, just in case. And everything was of the very poorest quality. Of course the lack of food and clothing was something to get used to, but there were restrictions on personal liberty with harsh prison sentences for speaking, evenly mildly, against the political communist regime. They refused to allow the ordinary citizen to travel outside the country's borders, except for privileged Party members. And so on, and so on. By the end they were standing up and cheering, asking for more. One thing that surprised them, when it was generally believed by most people, not just these prisoners, that in a

Communist state most people were Communists, it was not true as the maximum Party membership was never greater than 5%. They were also surprised that 5% in the right hands was enough to keep a state under absolute totalitarian control.

Then followed over an hour of questions covering a wide canvas, ranging from Anglo-American politics to the prevalence of drug taking in London. The most unexpected questions were about the London Theatre and, in [particular, John Osborne's works. The play "Look Back in Anger" was known to several of the cons and they wanted to know how it had changed out of all recognition the tempo and content of the modern theatre.

It was humbling talking to these men, most of whom would never walk outside a prison wall again, never climb a hill, smell a bank of wild flowers, feel the wind or, for God's sake, even the rain or snow on their faces. It is no use trying to understand what passes through the minds of such men. Even the warders cannot know and they, themselves, are prisoners of a sort over a long working day.

That, nevertheless, completed my stay in Baltimore. Having met Frankel, seen the people in thrall to him and learnt a lot about the unspoken business side of civil engineering, American style with its close links to politics, not in a million years could I ever have become part of it. It would be priggish to say it was a question of ethics, honesty and respect for people that decided that I should not become a player. Before even considering those aspects I know, and my wife knew, I was not suited to the life that would follow if I decided to work for Frankel. He wanted a 100% company man, of the sort that, to me, had always been an intellectual impossibility. Acting as a go-between, the company on one side, corrupt congressmen, local politicians and corrupt suppliers and building inspectors on the other? The matter was never mentioned, other than by Jimmy Swartz, but he said that a salary of $50,000 a year would be offered to me. This was an enormous sum in 1964, about £25,000, but what a pound of flesh would be required in justification.

At the outset it had been clear that my U.K. commitments, though not unbreakable, would make a move to America difficult. So we said our goodbyes and next day I flew to Detroit for the Exhibition and home three days after that. A long discussion with my wife followed. She was quite unequivocal, such a job was out of character and we would be divorced within a year. Thus closed the most bizarre episode of my business life.

Postscript

A month later a letter arrived from the Governor of Maryland State Penitentiary, effusive in his thanks for my lecture, and enclosing a brass key made in the prison workshop bearing on it the inscription "The key to Maryland State Penitentiary". A month after that there was a riot and five in the prison, two warders and three prisoners, were killed.

In January 1965 Winston Churchill died. Jimmy Swartz got a seat in St. Paul's Cathedral, representing the Governor of Maryland. We did not meet as I was out of the country but a week later he wrote to me asking if I would go to the grave, which is in the Churchyard of Bladon village just outside Woodstock, and take a set of photos for him. On a beautiful day, unusually fine and sunny for February, I stood at the foot of the grave. It was about nine thirty and nobody else was there. It was the closest I ever got to the greatest Englishman who ever lived.

YUGOSLAVIA

THEY MADE A DESERT AND CALLED IT PEACE

Jossip Broz-Tito displayed outstanding courage when, in 1948, he broke with Russia and, in a few years, turned the country from being the basket case of the Balkans into a single state. Tito, a Croat of the minor state of Croatia, persuaded the largest of the six states, Serbia, to join as an equal with the other five smaller countries. God knows what would have happened had he not succeeded. We read about the brave partisans who fought the Germans but, in truth, the Serbians and the Croats killed, tortured and massacred more of each other than they did of the Germans. True or false, the number of dead in the unofficial Civil War is never put at less than half a million, and that out of a population of no more than twenty millions. To weld together two peoples whose hatred of each other was immeasurable was the act of a genius, a conciliator of the highest order and in a few years, despite the constant threat of Russia and their Iron Curtain satellites, the united country displayed a confidence that attracted worldwide support. Tito was no less a Communist than Stalin but a national, not an international, sort.

Not that one should have expected unity of the six autonomous states to last much beyond the death of Tito, but he succeeded until 1980, after nearly forty years as leader. Now Yugoslavia is broken up again and I have as much confidence in the restoration of peace amongst that jumble of different peoples as I have of peace in Ireland or Palestine.

I first went there in 1957, after the usual gathering of industrial intelligence from various Embassies and agencies and the agreement of my American boss, who, as I expected, trusted my judgement in seeking out business in the most unpromising places. A potential agent had been contacted and we were to meet in Zagreb before moving on to the capital Belgrade. With four years of hard driving in Europe behind me the thousand miles to Belgrade could be faced with confidence. After a day in Belgium and Holland I drove from Charleroi, across Germany using the autobahnen to Nuremberg, Regenberg, Salzberg in Austria then South East to Graz and South to cross over into Croatia at the Austrian border village of Spielfeld. By that time, after 650 miles I was seeing double and needed a bed and food. A few miles over the border in a place called Jareninski, I saw what looked like an inn, perhaps like an Austrian inn ten miles behind me (the place had been Austrian pre-1914). Anyway I had had enough so I went in to be met by the innkeeper. I asked if he had a room, he said "How will you be paying, Sir?" "What to you want?" I replied, "Pounds, Marks, Schillings, Dollars?" "Yes there is a room, follow me". Up a rickety staircase we went, me first, and I pushed against a door partly opened. The first thing to catch my eye was a pair of boots sticking out from the bottom of a bed. The boss pushed past me, pulled a blanket from off a fully clad body, grabbed said body roughly by the shoulders and heaved it out of the bed, out of the room and into the corridor. "There you are, Sir, that will be two dollars when you come down to breakfast." Such was my fatigue I was unmoved by this cavalier treatment of mine host to a former guest that I just climbed onto the bed and went to sleep, like a thief in the night.

Next morning there was water for washing, then a breakfast of stale bread, coffee and slivovitz, which I refused. What a marvellous welcome from a country that was to see a lot of me in the next six years.

Belgrade was an old, dusty broken-down Balkan town, half destroyed by bombing during the German invasion of April 1941. The Turkish 400 years of occupation had left little visual evidence of its presence, save the cobbled roads. Cobbles the size of cricket balls over which only a tank could comfortably pass. Yet there were no food shortages and the people were reasonably clad. Still, they did have a Grand Hotel of the old style, the Beograd. Serbia was never part of the old Austro-Hungarian Empire, its influence had been considerable, so in the big towns, Sarajevo, Skopkje and a few others there was always one hotel that offered a comfortable bed, bath and dinner. Most of my sorties into Yugoslav industry began and ended at the Beograd, and it was only five minutes walk to my agent's office, Machinokomerc. It was, of course, a Government organisation which by acting as agents for foreign companies, such as mine, allowed them to skim 10% off the top of a successful sale as commission. But the relationship between its people and me was a good one, and without Machinokomerc my penetration into the Yugoslav foundry industry, especially into the military foundries, would have been immensely difficult and the next six years much less profitable.

Beginning in 1957 there was a great relaxation in foreign trade. Tito realising the need for capital plant, encouraged trade links with the West, to replace the archaic equipment of the 1930's. No help or anything came from Moscow. Tito was a pariah, a traitor, a running dog of the USA and the UK, or so the propaganda spewed out daily on Radio Moscow said. In short, I could not have chosen a better time to come. My masters were very pleased with me.

There were few cars, nor many bicycles either. A feature of all Communist countries, and Yugoslavia was still Communist, was the use of trams and buses, all very old and over-used. Which is why the working day was always single shift, 0600 to 1400 hours, and as nobody went home to lunch there were only two peak travel periods instead of four.

During the next 18 months I motored down every 10 weeks and stayed from two to three weeks, visiting many foundries from Zagreb in the North the capital of Croatia, to Skopje in the South the capital of Macedonia, mostly accompanied by my agent Mikael Jelic, since little but Serbo-Croat was spoken. Many foundries from big to very big were visited, lectures were given, work practices analysed and the best of Western technology discussed. But it was twelve months before the sniff of an order wafted our way. Patience, massive patience, is required when dealing with government beaurocracy. For every penny spent came from the Treasury coffers in Belgrade. The first order is rather like seeding rain clouds with dry ice – it can be followed by a deluge of serious interest and more orders. A foundry in Krusevac started to make promising noises and wanted a meeting at their Belgrade headquarters to discuss a quotation which had been submitted and changed several times over the last year. The foundry was so primitive it would have been better to bulldoze it flat and start with a green field site. In fact, although I did not know it, that was the intention. An experimental cum production foundry to make tank components was to be erected alongside the old foundry with the intention in due course to treble the area and the output.

The meeting started at 0700 and I was faced with six engineers from Krusevac, three bodies from the Trade Ministry and a girl interpreter who only spoke German, and my agent. My boss had given me a firm instruction not to give any discount above 5%. Intelligence from several sources had intimated that no other supplier was under consideration, and provided a price and delivery which was acceptable, the order was mine. We went over all the ground covered in six previous meetings at the foundry, and we analysed every line in the twenty page quotation which had been in their hands for six months. We talked round the only reason I was there, which was money. So for a further two hours we haggled. That was the word and, in the end, I gave a discount of three and a quarter percent on an order worth, near enough at the time, 200,000 dollars, a very large amount fortysix years ago. In addition I said my company would train two of their engineers in Cleveland for a month when the equipment was nearing completion and undergoing trials. That swung it. My boss had not made any such offer but I was confident he would back me in that which he did. They also accepted severe terms of payment. During the six hours a Turkish coffee with a slivovitz arrived every twenty minutes. By 1.30pm I was almost beyond speech, not from Slivovitz, but from talking and exhaustion. My agent helped me to the Beograd, only 200 yards away. I went to bed and remained there until 6 o'clock next morning. Joy, as they say in my Cleveland office, was unconfined.

From this eighteen months of spade work substantial orders covering a wide variety of plant were received from foundries in Novisad, Banjaluka, Sarajevo, Niz, Skopje and Kikinda. That town stands out in my memory. It was near to the Romanian border, 60 miles North East of Belgrade, and the nearer you got to the town the more primitive were the surroundings. Romania, of course, was the most poverty-stricken area of the Balkans. I made five visits to Kikinda in eight months, twice alone and despite an almost complete absence of traffic, the state of the road was so bad that the 60 miles took four hours to do. The dust was so bad, that all windows had to be shut, in a temperature of 90 degrees F. and still the dust got in. Twice I broke back axle springs, and twice had them repaired in Kikinda for about a couple of quid each time. Villages were squalid, houses were hovels, and there were flocks of geese everywhere. I recall a woman, a Muslim for she was veiled, walking along a hedgerow and spinning round and round a hand held spindle using sheep's wool gathered from the hedge.

Equally primitive was the town of Niz, about 100 miles South of Belgrade at which I arrived on Friday night. You could tell the day by the thickness of the men's beards – Sunday was shaving day. After taking my kit to my room I went down to eat. A gypsy string band was playing those Balkan tunes which sound more Arab than Western. My feet slipped on the grease covered floor and, as I sat down, a waiter, or rather THE waiter, produced a wine glass. He had just taken it out of a bowl of water and, sensing the presence of an English Milord, dried it with his dirty handkerchief, or rather snot rag, and filled it with the stomach wrenching red wine which I tolerated for there was no other. He then pulled from his rear pocket a dirty piece of paper, the menu, written in Serbo-Croat and the Cyrillic script which I did not understand. So I stood up, went over to other occupied tables and showed the waiter what he should bring. This is quite easy when you have done it from one end of Yugoslavia to the other. A little more wine and a slivovitz or two and I went to bed, if only to escape the gypsy band.

At about two in the morning there was a hell of a row coming from next door, banging and screaming, and hurried footsteps from down below, where the band was still belting out some dirge. I poked my head out of the door to see a ball of fire disappear down the staircase, followed by two naked figures, both men. Ah well! It happens all the time, I suppose. A bloke had gone to sleep, probably drunk, with a fag in his mouth which set a mattress on fire, which woke me up highly amused.

Later that day it was pleasant to be back at the Hotel Beograd. One thing I was never short of was books. I never had less than half a dozen with me for, inevitably, there were long periods of inactivity, especially at night and weekends. I had brought with me Michael Foot's biography of Aneurin Bevan. In the lounge after dinner, having just finished it, I started on Jane Austin's "Sense and Sensibility", a book I re-read from time to time, and one I am sure not observed often in a Balkan hotel on a Saturday night. Engrossed in what is a damn good read I looked up to find all the comfortable chairs and sofas occupied by very smartly dressed girls, clearly the pick of the Belgrade "ladies of the night". What a book to be reading in their presence. Jane Austin, not an unworldly woman, would have been amused.

Slovenia is a beautiful country and its capital is Ljubjana, a handsome Austro-Hungarian town. Mostly I travelled there from Italy, having first stopped off in Venice to buy newspapers and black currency, for the same reason I bought it before entering any of the Communist states, it reduced the cost of travel admirably. The countryside from the border to Ljubjana is undulating with white rocky outcrops amidst clumps of heather, not unlike the South West of Ireland. Slovenia used to be called Styria under the Austrians and Pannonia under the Romans.

The Slon hotel in Ljubjana could have been in the Tyrol, and I was always pleased to stay there. On this first visit I was sitting in the lounge with a beer when a tall, very old, beaky nosed imperious sort of woman, stamped in, leaning on a stick and yelling what seemed to be orders in Serbo-Croat to a nervous waiter. Seeing me, she came across to observe more closely an obvious stranger, for this was Mrs. Copeland, a resident in the hotel since the 1930's. The newspaper I was reading might, of course, have given her a clue as to what or who I was. We talked amiably enough though she gave no information about herself. Probing other people I learned she had come out from England first as a nanny to a minor member of the Yugoslavian Royal family, and then had stayed on in other capacities. Like English nannies the world over she terrified the natives. She certainly bossed over the Slon hotel servants. And, I was told, the Germans during World War II.

Some months later, I had the managing director (for want of a better description) of the Niz foundry with whom I was in negotiation in London. Thinking to impress him with the Mother of Parliaments I took him to see a debate in the House of Commons. It was a minor debate but a reasonably full House. Now this was a man who, during the German occupation, had probably seen or even taken part in a massacre or two. When he saw members of both front benches with their feet up on the table (for this was 1962) he was shocked by such lack of respect.

In late July of 1963, alone, I had motored South of Skopje in Macedonia to a town near the border of Greece. I intended to stay the night in Skopje on my way back but I changed my mind and continued to Niz to the hotel in which I had witnessed the bedroom fire. That night, or rather at 5 o'clock in the morning of July 26th 1963 Skopje was half destroyed by a violent earthquake. There were over a thousand dead and more than three thousand wounded.

Except for a visit to Zpenjanin in December of that year I was never in Yugoslavia again.

Always a poor country, it had made great strides in improving the condition of the people while Tito was alive. He died in 1980 and was hardly cold in his grave before Croatia and Serbia were at each other's throats. In 1990 the next Civil War started with Serbs killing Croats and both killing the Muslim Bosnians. Kosovo joined in later and that massacre was worse than that of 1941/2/3.

The Balkans, or what was Yugoslavia, (except for Slovenia, Montenegro and Macedonia) is a basket case once more. There will not be real peace in my lifetime. It will be the peace of Palestine, no more, no less. Don't our politicians read ANY history?

HUNGARY

IF YOU GO INTO A REVOLVING DOOR,

AND THE MAN BEHIND YOU COMES OUT IN FRONT OF YOU,

HE IS PROBABLY HUNGARIAN

My visits were fewer than those to other Communist bloc states, but just as memorable. Following on the Polish uprising of early 1956, Moscow was panicking at the loud muttering amongst the Hungarian dissidents. The Party Secretary, Gero, who had hanged his predecessor Rakossi, who in turn had hanged his predecessor (strange how a Revolution always consumes its own) got the wind up and asked the Russians in Budapest to do something. The Russians, initially not quite knowing what to do, retreated from the town. On, I think, October 22nd 1956, and on my way to Budapest, I turned on the radio and tuned in to the Austrian radio to hear that the Russians were moving back. I was about twenty miles from the capital and thought it best to go back to Vienna. On the night of the 23rd they came in mob handed with tanks, infantry and the KGB, and virtually put the town to the sword. Over three thousand people were killed, with an unknown number executed, and two hundred thousand people fled over the open frontiers of Austria to the great benefit of the various Western nations, including the UK, in which they settled. A clever lot the Hungarians, like the Czechs. Many Hungarians believed that Russia only dared to attack Budapest because it could be done under cover of the world's greater pre-occupation with the Israeli-Franco-British invasion of Egypt to protect the Suez Canal from being taken over. It failed and brought down Anthony Eden the Prime Minister.

Imre Nagy, the new Party Secretary and a man of un-Stalinist sympathies had replaced Gero, and sought refuge in the Yugoslav Embassy. In 1958, on the promise of safe conduct, he came out and was promptly hanged.

It was 1960 before I went again, but was not having the same success there as I was having in Czechoslovakia and Yugoslavia. The German firms had got Hungary well and truly sewn up. Still, one had to keep on trying. Budapest was a great gathering place for international salesmen (or sales executives, as one must now call them). Most of them drank heavily whilst whingeing on about lack of support from their respective head-quarters, especially the British. The main boozing spot was the bar in the Gellert Hotel, which was absolutely magnificent, in Buda across the Danube from Pest. Budapest is really two towns divided by the river. It was (and continues to be) a microcosm of Austro-Hungarian opulence.

There was one man I saw several times in the Gellert who was usually with a Hungarian, rather than the Brits. Just the once he chatted with me, a very interesting man who spent most of his time in the Communist bloc states, including Russia, selling equipment made by his British principals. He was the agent for a number of companies, and his name was Greville Wynne. On Friday the 2nd of November 1962 he was bundled into a car outside his hotel and next day was in the Moscow Lubianka Prison. After five months in the Lubianka under intensive interrogation during which he refused to confess to espionage, he was put on trial along with his Russian contact Colonel Oleg Penkovsky, Wynne received five years and Penkovsky was shot for treason. After eleven months in a Russian prison where he was treated with great harshness, short of food, beaten and with periods in solitary confinement, he was released in exchange for Gordon Lonsdale, the Russian spy serving a long sentence in England.

Hungary was always a pleasant place to be and, except for the usual border strictness, Budapest could have been in almost any Western country. The food was good and the people reasonably well dressed. There was, of course, the usual complaint that they were not allowed to travel outside the Communist bloc and only within it with difficulty. At the Opera once, to see Beethoven's Fidelio, the audience was as well dressed as they would have been at Covent Garden. Political jokes were on everybody's lips and, as in Warsaw, you could say what you liked about the Russians, but not about the Government.

During the Russian invasion of October 1956, the Catholic Cardinal Mindszenty retreated to the American Embassy where he remained until well into the l980's. To ensure there was no attempt at escape the Secret Police stationed a car outside the Embassy, always in exactly the same place. This car became a tourist attraction. Not the car itself so much as the ten-foot diameter patch of oil underneath it from years of dripping oil from clapped out engines. I saw it in 1963, the last year I was in Hungary for business.

Postscript

In the Spring of 1990 I paid a valedictory visit to Budapest. The Berlin Wall was down and Hungary was in the throes of becoming a democracy. One reason I went was to find the grave of Imre Nagy. He had been thrown into a common grave along with others who had also been hanged, but his body had been exhumed and re-buried with full International Honours. It took over three hours and sixty dollars in taxi fares to find the grave, beside which I stood alone. Nobody seemed to know who I was talking about, as I asked where I could find the grave of Imre Nagy – of course, I should have said "Nagy Imre" as in Hungary the patronymic is always said before the Christian name.

CZECHOSLOVAKIA

"GOOD MORNING, SIR. I AM FROM THE GOVERNMENT

AND I AM HERE TO HELP YOU"

In the U.S.A. such a call on a man who has been less than truthful when completing his tax return might perhaps have given him a minor attack of the collywobbles. When it happened in Czechoslovakia and the visit was made by a couple of heavies in the early hours, say 3a.m., it was more likely to cause a heart attack, and not for any fiddling of your taxes. A long prison sentence was the least to be expected. After the Communist Party took power forcibly in 1948, having lost an election, that unhappy country was no place to be living in if you were not a Party member, were of middle class, out of the country in the U.K. during the War, a doctor or what was venomously called bourgeois.

How did one get to Czechoslovakia in September 1958? Firstly you needed a visa (money, much form filling, plus three photographs) and then, in my case, I drove there. I set out from Lindfield in West Sussex (my home) at 2100 hours on a Sunday night, West to East through the narrow winding roads of East Sussex and Kent, through Crowborough, Mark Cross, Wadhurst, Goudhurst, Ashford, Sellindge and Folkstone to the Dover Eastern Dock. It was like driving in the wartime blackout, it was so dark and the villages had little or no lighting once the many pubs were shut. Shut? I was once told that if your hearing was very acute, the chink of glasses could be heard long after chucking out time. I was doing all this to catch a Belgian rust bucket of a ferry called the Queen Astrid at midnight, which dumped you on the Ostend dockside at 04.30. How many times did I make that journey before the M25 was built? Countless times and why did I do it? I suppose I was keen, ambitious and hungry and wanted to get out, get on with it and get back home.

So there you are in the streets of Ostend, where you could still smell the chips and moules mariniéres from the Saturday night feasting, with the dead straight road to Bruxelles, all 117 kilometres of it, ahead. After an hour, and an easy passage through Bruxelles at that time, I went on to Louvain, Charleroi, Liége (all the names were actually in Flemish), across the River Meuse and then on to Aachen (Aix la Chapelle). This was Charlemagne's capital in 800A.D. All the cobbled roads were like driving on half bricks but from Aachen, where began the German autobahnen what great joy! It was like driving on a billiard table and I continued thus the 500 miles to Munich, a driving hellhole, for there you needed to go through the town. It is said, by the haughty citizens of Hamburg, that the Bavarian shopkeepers of Munich, who result from the crossing of an Austrian with a human being, obstinately delayed the motor road round the town on the premise that he who drives round a town does not spend money in it. It was another twenty years before the by-pass was built. An hour was lost but then the Autobahn started again, all eighty miles across the Austrian border to Salzburg, and on to Linz (the birthplace of Hitler) and the partly constructed Austrian motor road to Vienna. There was no time to admire the lovely hilly countryside around Steyr, the inspiration of so much music by Schubert. Fourteen hours after getting off the boat I reached the centre of Vienna and there the Hotel Graben, a litre of beer and a huge wienershnitzel brought me back to life – and sleep – in a bath – for there was no room at the inn. The Hotel was full, but the owner, whom I knew for the next thirty years, took pity on me and found me a bath in which to sleep. The whole town was full as Vienna was very short of hotels and remained so for some years.

850 miles in a day, which was the distance from Ostend to Vienna, is not difficult provided you are a diligent and road wise driver, take with you two bottles of unsweetened and unmilked strong tea, have a comfortable bladder and, most important of all, drive alone.

Down to Gehenna or up to the Throne,
He travels fastest who travels alone.

Next morning, refreshed and with not even a back ache from the bath, and stopping only at the nearest bank to change Austrian schillings into Czech crowns at a rate six times better than the official Czech rate, I set out North for my first trip behind the iron curtain. I never played ball with the Communist States on this currency game. They knew their currencies were all but useless when exposed to the open market. They must have known also that there were plenty of subversives such as yours truly who were unwilling to play according to their rules. Yet they did nothing, until about 1980 when hotel bills had to be paid in hard currency. Even then, the fluttering of a one dollar bill in the face of a reception clerk would get you a room, however full a hotel claimed to be.

My destination was Brno (Brün in German), a very old Bohemian town in the province of Moravia, part of the old Austro-Hungarian Empire, and before that of the ancient Holy Roman Empire. A lovely baroque town, it had been untouched by war since the 30 Years' War of 1618 – 1648. The frontier is at Mikulov about 40 miles of the 80 to Brno, and long before reaching that point you felt the Balkans were about you. The villages became shabbier and the roads were unpaved. It was almost as if the Austrians had decided that if the Russians attacked from Brno why bother to spend money on repairs?

There was no physical barrier at the Austrian crossing, only a customs man to wave you on, snug in his little hut. Then there was a nomansland for about a mile before one reached the first barrier, a red and white painted steel girder embedded in concrete, guarded, of course, but liftable to let cars through. At a further 400 yards there was a menacing barrier at which your passport was taken. At one side was the Customs House and on the other a thirty feet high watchtower, complete with an armed guard with rifle and powerful searchlight. To left and right, as far as the eye could see, was a triple barrier, nine feet high, of barbed wire with areas of ploughed soil on either side for fifty yards. This soil was full of mines and trip wires.

This was a dramatic moment and a traumatic experience, but one with which I was to become familiar over the next twenty years. To read about this was one thing, but to see it? Winston Churchill gave a speech at Fulton, Missouri on 5th March 1946 in which he said "From Stettin in the Baltic to Trieste in the Adriatic an iron curtain has descended across the Continent." He was speaking metaphorically, as the Russian takeover had not yet begun. Now I was standing in front of the physical Iron Curtain, which extended over 2,000 miles from North to South. Over the years I saw the despair in the faces of the East Germans, Poles, Czechs and Hungarians as they saw this monstrous barrier between tyranny and liberty. This first meeting with the border mix of customs, police and soldiers took no longer than thirty minutes. There was a reason for this brevity. An Exhibition was about to begin in Brno and hundreds of foreigners were crossing borders instead of handfuls.

We were to remember each other's faces on and off over the years when, perhaps in the depths of winter, I was alone at the crossing and the boredom could be relieved by a minute examination of my baggage and, should the spirit move them, a part dismantlement of my car. Surprisingly there was never a body search. It could have been much worse and, in a way, it was comforting to recognise the same unfriendly faces when moving from West to East. My dossier with the Political Police must have been fat before they decided I really was what I claimed to be, a bona fide businessman. So the minor humiliations of border crossing were more annoying that menacing. In my kit I always carried twenty or so packs of fags and several half bottles of scotch. If things started to get stroppy they helped wonderfully. I would also leave lying about several current copies of Austrian newspapers and magazines, which were always picked up furtively – an interesting act of mild subversion.

Brno had been an important holder of Exhibitions in the manner of Leipzig and Hanover for hundreds of years, and I was on my way to the annual International Mechanical and Engineering Exhibition that was to run for three weeks, which was an extraordinary length. In the West an Exhibition was usually for one week but in a Communist State three weeks was not unusual as it brought in thousands of foreigners spending millions of greatly needed hard currency. It was important to the Government, but to the people it was a gift of immeasurable delight for they could meet, often for the first time, foreigners, people as difficult to encounter as aliens from outer space. The only Czechs who were allowed to travel were Party Members, five per cent of the population, and even they had to leave their families behind as a guarantee of their return.

Before 1939 the Czechs had one of the highest standards of living in

Europe, one of the largest middle classes and highest of education standards. It was a stable democracy until, in 1938, the Germans marched in. They had none of the poverty of Poland, Russia, Hungary and the rest of Eastern Europe. Their engineers built part of the London Underground and designed the Bren machine guns and other weapons that were standard in the British and other armies. But they were considered bourgeois, a terrible curse in the eyes of a Marxist.

The crowds who attended rivalled that of a local derby between Aston Villa and Birmingham or Arsenal and Chelsea. Our pavilion was circular and people were shoulder to shoulder, round and round, all day between opening at nine o'clock and closing at six. They were not customers but gawkers, looking at foreigners and how they were dressed and shod. I was there as my American company's representative and to help the British company who built our machines under license, several of which were being exhibited. Beyond that I was meeting engineers of the various Czech nationalised foundries to discuss projects under consideration. Our penetration up until the Russian invasion in August 1968 was considerable. Thereafter it was nothing.

We were a friendly lot, British, French, German, Scandinavian and others. Friends together, competitors, but we were united, as it were, in enemy territory. One evening at about 5 o'clock, tired after hours of talking, I sat down, put my feet on a table with a glass of whisky in one hand and started to read a recent copy of The Times. The eyes of the passersby observing this stood out on stalks, and they laughed, nudging one another. I was the living proof of the arrogant, insolent capitalist dog that their political masters were always telling them about. It made their day. The news got around and people came to our Stand to view and enjoy this prime example of Western living, and did us no harm at all. So I did it most days, like a freak show at a circus, with the same newspaper but fresh whisky for we had it by the case. Friendships were made and I have been in touch with one Czech for fortyfive years whom I met at that first occasion in Brno in 1958.

My hotel, even by the shaky standards of Eastern Europe, was grotty. I shared with another bloke, a friend, and our beds were end to end – it was that sort of a room. My head at night felt as though it was in an oven, because the chimney leading up from the kitchen was two inches from my pillow and was so hot it was untouchable with the bare hand. In the bathroom the hot tap ran scalding water at about a cupful a minute and the cold tap nothing at all. The food was not uninteresting, especially to the chap who ordered a schnitzel, put his knife under the crisp crumb coating to disclose a perfectly formed pig's ear. It was a pork schnitzel. On the other hand another man, a German, came in latish one night bag in one hand and a pair of hares in the other. On an empty country road in full moonlight and driving fast he could not avoid killing a pair of copu-lating hares. The hotel cook knew what to do and served up jugged hare two days later.

This was no ordinary Exhibition, it was an experience granted to few. Our interpreter was a water colourist with a developing reputation as a painter of opera backcloths, a student of the great Kokotchka. Because we were Anglos the Stand became a meeting place for writers, journalists, university students and others just wanting to talk with someone from beyond the wire. They all had certain things in common, middle class, well educated, low paid jobs (well below their abilities), and children, if they had any, were denied university places because their parents were not of the proletariat, or Party Members. Oddly enough, as I write, the same bias against English middle class children is being practised by New Labour if they are foolish enough to have attended independent or public schools. What did Marx say about history repeating itself?

These people were under constant surveillance and several were im-prisoned after the Russians invaded in 1968. The people who I felt even more sorry for were the elderly who suffered under the Germans from 1938 to 1945 and then, after three years of liberty, under the Communists. They had endured a slave state for nearly twenty years and were not to gain liberty for another thirty. By God! Do the British really appreciate their good fortune? Somebody once said that to be born English was to win the lottery of life.

There were parties with out Czech friends, and food they could ill afford, but plenty of good but cheap wine from the nearby vineyards. Bitter political jokes were exchanged and sometimes dangerous talk was voiced. At a party in an ancient wine cellar when the wine was running freely and tongues were loosening, a joke was told which ended with "Heil Hitler". In attendance was the village policeman, very drunk and regarded as 'one of us'. On hearing the "Heil Hitler" he drew his gun, emptied it into the roof and burst into tears. Nobody had known that the Germans had hanged his father in 1942.

We left Brno after nearly four weeks, happy with our new friends. But as I was to be in Brno, Prague and many other towns over the next eleven years we never lost touch. One man in particular, Vaclav Novak, had been a soldier in the Czech Brigade, formed in the U.K. in 1940, and on returning in 1946 received the usual bad treatment at the hands of the Communists. To have served with the British marked you as tainted by capitalism and, therefore, dangerous. He asked me and, perhaps foolishly, I agreed to deliver several audio tapes to his friends in Reading. Fortunately the Mikulov frontier crossing was busy and I received little attention; some whisky changed hands.

Over the next few years I brought out various pieces of jewelry which a friend in the U.S.A. had asked me to bring out from his uncle, a classics professor at the Charles University in Prague. I also smuggled out, if smuggled is the right word, something much larger and which aroused more amusement than suspicion at the frontier. It was a cast iron motor cylinder crankcase of a tractor engine. I was engaged in advanced negotiation for a large order to make engine components for the State Tractor Foundry in Brno. The value of the order was about £500,000 and time could be saved in designing the tools if our designers could have a specimen block. So I decided to bring one back with me – on the front passenger seat of my Jaguar. It weighed 150 lbs. To save any trouble at border crossings in Austria, Germany, Belgium or France with long winded explanations, I only crossed them in the early hours of the morning. The journey took four days instead of two and a half but the effort was worth it. Customs people can be stroppy when faced with something they don't recognise.

In 1961/2 there was a bitter joke, based on fact, told all over Czechoslovakia which, in order to understand it, one needed to know the relationship between Vienna and Brno. For many generations the two cities would be spoken of in the same breath. They were but seventy miles apart, which is the point of the story, and there was much intermarriage. When the railway link was built and the car became common there would be much coming and going between families. They were like Siamese twins joined at the hip. So the closing of the frontier by the Communists was a terrible thing. Passes to go from one to the other were difficult to obtain and families were sometimes cut off for years. In 1961 Yuri Gagarin, the Russian Cosmonaut, became the first man to circumnavigate the earth in space. Russia and its client states were triumphant. A Russian patriot had beaten the Americans to achieve this greatest of scientific feats. Gagarin was sent off on a lecture tour to all the Warsaw Pact countries as a propaganda exercise to put America's nose out of joint. He talked of what he had done, and the superiority of Russian space technology over that of America. And he *may* have even given the impression that any citizen of our great and glorious Russian Empire would one day be able to fly thousands of miles through space. And then questions were due to be asked. In Brno, it is said, there was a deathly hush, then a small voice asked from the back of the lecture hall "Please Mr. Gagarin, when can we go to Vienna?"

In 1964 I parted with my American employers to set up my own company, and l965 found me back on my old European stamping grounds in the countries I had opened up to my American Company. Every two months or so I was in Czechoslovakia where the Cold War ensured no political change. Until 1967 that is. The murmurs of dissent were getting louder and a defiant mood was gathering strength. In 1967 Alexander Dubcek replaced Antonin Novotny, the Soviet stooge, as General Secretary of the Party. He was younger, thought differently and wanted more freedom of action, some freedom for the media, and even, perhaps, freedom to travel. Then began in January 1968 the "Prague Spring", and "Socialism with a Smiling Face". The people were joyful and full of hope. From then on, and to my astonishment, the border police at Mikulov and other crossing points, who had for years given me a hard time, now started shaking my hand, asking me how I was keeping, making me coffee. Back in Moscow, Brezhnev was going berserk, remembering Hungary in 1956, and was having none of it.

In February of that year, with snow and ice the whole way from

Frankfort, I reached Brno in my new fantasy motor. When a man is not too far off fifty he is inclined to do silly things like get a new wife, or, in my case, a dream car. A car that no man should drive doing my mileage. Perhaps it should have been driven gently over the weekend, or into the countryside for a picnic, but not all over Europe in all weathers. I bought a Mini Cooper 'S' with two fuel tanks, two Stromberg one and a half inch diameter carburetors, high lift camshaft and tuned by Mr. Downton of Southampton who was greatly skilled in the putting of quarts into pint pots. It was only 1300cc capacity but developed 138 brake horse power, accelerated from 0 – 60mph in seven seconds, with a top speed of 135mhp. And there was another thing – it would not function on petrol of less than 98 octane. In Eastern Europe the octane was 70. Which, blended with the smell of brown coal stank the streets of Czechoslovakia et al. So as not to risk having to fill my tanks East of Mikulov, I took with me two jerricans of fuel, 12 gallons carried on the back seats. To all intents and purposes I was driving a bomb – it would be best not to hit anything!

When I arrived in Brno, the pavements were still covered with December's snow and the temperature was −15°C. I parked outside the Grand Hotel, my pull-up since 1960 and quite splendid in the old Austro-Hungarian way. The waiters still wore dinner jackets and the Maître d'Hotel, evening dress, an odd eccentricity in the egalitarian Communist State but encouraged, I believe, by the political masters. Next morning I went outside and saw twenty or thirty young men gathered round my car, for the like had not been seen in Brno before. Not wishing to lose a chance of showing off British technology I raised the bonnet and revved the engine, which sounded like a Formula I. The lads clapped in appreciation and one of them came over. I knew who he was for we had met at one of our parties in 1958. We had called him Geoff because his Czech name was difficult. He knew me too and had a broad grin on his face. A short talk followed on old times and he said, "You were right, you know," in almost flawless English. I was puzzled but didn't want to betray my ignorance." You were right when you said 'Freedom from tyranny can only be achieved from inside of a country, not from outside' and now we are going to get it." There were tears in his eyes and damn nearly in mine too – the things one says when drunk! Truly, in vino veritas.

What a pity it was a false Dawn, or should I say false Spring. He, my friends and the millions of people in tragic Czechoslovakia had to wait a further twentyone years. I drove east to the Tatra Mountains, and I never met Geoff again.

Moving forward a few months, on, I think, August 16th after completing some business in Manchester, it was opportune to stay at a small country house hotel on Lake Ullswater in the Lake District called Sharrow Bay. Its owners, two men, were wartime RAF comrades of a neighbour of mine, who had long suggested I stay there, and so I did. It was all my friends said it was with good food, comfort and nice people. But the time spent there was short and I left at 0500 next morning to go home, for in 48 hours I should be back on the old milk run to Prague and Brno. You may wonder how I remember this date after an interval of thirtyfive years. Sharrow quickly earned an international reputation and today is considered, by those who claim to know about these things, to be one of the greatest of country hotels.

On the 18th I set off but, because my destination was Prague, I went by way of Nuremberg, crossing into Czechoslovakia at Rozvadov to Pilzen and on to Prague, before travelling east to Ostrava near the Polish border to the Tatra Motor Company, hoping to collect a substantial order which had taken a year of complicated negotiations and many visits to get and would, I felt sure, be only the first of many and my company would receive the status of "Preferential Supplier". On the afternoon of the 20th, with my car parked outside, the Alcron Hotel was once more my temporary Prague pad – for the last time as I was to discover a few hours later. After a dinner of the usual stodgy fare (it is possible to have dumplings with just about every course in Prague, from hors d'oeuvres to dessert) I was in bed by 11 o'clock. In the early hours there was pandemonium, shouting, screaming and heavy footsteps, so I got up and dressed. The Russians had landed in strength on the Airport and Warsaw Pact troops, East Germans, Poles, Hungarians and Bulgarians, had crossed the frontiers from the north, south, east and west. Clearly this was more than a rumour and radios were switched on loudly all over the place. The Prague Spring had been short lived, Communism with a smiling face had been no more than a forced rictus, and I got the hell out of Prague, packed up, paid up and left the city going due east, i.e. 180° from the Airport in the direction of Ostrava. Many trucks full of Polish infantry passed me accompanied by artillery and tanks. I calculated their number as being at least two divisions which must have crossed the frontier at Ciezyn. They did not look happy. The Tatra people had not forgotten about my visit, but were not a little surprised to see me. The atmosphere was calm, for centuries foreign armies had passed that way from the east, and they preferred Poles to Germans. Anyway they reckoned that action, if any, would be in Prague, not Ostrava. "As to business, forget it," the Manager said, "but don't forget us. No order can be placed, the one we had signed yesterday in readiness for your visit will be torn up." "Don't do that" I said "Give it to me as a souvenir, along with a letter of cancellation," which they did. It was still only mid-day. "Please come back" were their last words.

I stayed the night in Ostrava and next morning positioned myself just off the Prague Road, and made a count of military vehicles for a couple of hours, particularly of armour and artillery. A Polish officer approached me and we talked amiably enough. He spoke German and French and when I asked him, in all innocence, what it was all about, he said they had come to rescue their Czech comrades from the NATO army now massed on the Nuremberg-Rosvadov frontier point ready to attack the freedom loving socialist nations. I had the feeling that he talked that rubbish tongue in cheek but I didn't tell him I had passed through Rosvadov two days ago and seen nothing. Nuremberg was a big NATO/ USA base.

Later I motored west to Brno, booked into the Grand and strolled about in places I had known for years, trying to gauge people's feelings. The radio and TV were telling of unarmed attacks by brave young men on the Russian tanks in Wenceslas Square, climbing onto the tanks to talk to the terrified young conscripts who didn't seem to know they were in Prague, much less in Czechoslovakia.

Next morning I decided to go back to Prague rather than to Austria. So once again I stopped to observe and count vehicles of the Hungarian army which had come up from the south and was moving north towards Prague. The plan seemed to be to ring Prague but not to go in, while the Russians did the business there of putting Dubcek and his ministers in chains, sending them to Moscow to soften them up, and then to return them, full of remorse for their naughtiness. Which is exactly what happened. I took secondary roads north and east, and with no difficulty returned to the Alcron Hotel.

On this, the fourth day, the Russians seemed to have stopped shooting, at least I didn't hear any. The tanks were stationary and the young Czechs were still haranguing the tank crews. At the top of the Square, in a turning to the left, there was the Hotel Esplanade, normally full of journalists and their like in an extremely friendly bar so I strolled up to have a look. The journalists were there all right, BBC, ITV, The Times, The Telegraph, Sun, Mirror, etc. but they were, more or less, locked in and were forbidden to set a foot on the outside pavement by the cops. When they found out what I'd been doing and where doing it I was a very popular fellow. Their knowledge of the events of the past two days was sketchy until I arrived. After which they were able to telex or telephone tales of the invasion. I doubt if my name was mentioned in their dispatches. In fact, I'm not sure if they asked what it was. That same day the crackling voice of the last free, poignant broadcast from Radio Prague to the outside world was heard "Please remember Czechoslovakia when we are no longer in the news."

My return journey followed the same route as my inward, over the border at Rozvadov, where the police and customs were very nice to me, and on to Nuremberg. There was no evidence of NATO activity there. After World War II the Allies agreed with Soviet Russia on zones of influence, Czechoslovakia went to the Russians. Had the considerable NATO force at Nuremberg, which was 100% American, moved over the border at Rozvadov and did the forty miles to Pilzen the great industrial town cheered on by the Czechs all the way, the Warsaw Pact troops would certainly not have attacked them. Such a pre-emptive move, probably without a drop of blood being spilt, would have changed the shape of Europe twentytwo years earlier, and lessened the suffering of people who had had more than their fair share of suffering. Ever the optimist, I motored down again in January, but except for the pleasure of seeing friends in Brno it was a wasted journey. Business with the Czechs would be on hold for a long time, and the old nastiness at the Mikulov frontier was back with a vengeance.

Postscript

In January 1969 the young philosophy student, Jan Palach, as a protest against the rape of his country once more on August 21st 1968, set fire to himself in Wenceslas Square.

LOOKING BACK

WHEN YOU TRAVEL TAKE HALF AS MUCH CLOTHING AS YOU

THINK YOU MAY NEED, BUT TWICE AS MUCH MONEY

I was told that even now, in the U.K. there are people, not necessarily young, who have not travelled more than 10 miles from their place of birth, and are pretty damned pleased with themselves about it. It is not unusual to meet a Scouser or a Brummy who has never been to London. So why on earth did I take a decision to spend 40 or so years or so motoring, flying, on trains or, sometimes, buses? Clocking up more than 40,000 miles in some years and flying 20,000 miles or so in the same year? Enduring the discomfort of French pavé roads, Italian driving maniacs and Yugoslav roads which even 17th century England would have treated with disdain? Stomaching foul food (all food is not French) gut wrenching wines and, in Italy, stale bread on Sundays, because the Italians do not bake bread on Sundays? Well, of course, no decision was taken. I stumbled into it with the insouciance of the lunatic and a firm belief in that fellow who said "God looks after lunatics and bastards". I must check my birth certificate. There is no other answer. I elected to spend 7 – 8 months a year for 10 years almost like a gypsy or, as my eldest son said, the Flying Dutchman, doomed to drive down the roads of Europe for ever. Absences in the other years were bad but never as bad, and the mileage travelled not much less. Yet I have been married to the same woman for 57 years, who understands me perfectly, better than I do myself. Whatever success has come my way, either in life or work, has been influenced by her advice or criticism. On the few occasions when she strongly advised against my doing something on which I was apparently fixed, I bowed to her judgment. I loved, and love her, above all things. Her stoicism in the face of long absence was wonderful, with only the crudest methods of communication. Compare that with today when the modern woman demands the man must be home promptly on Friday night. Phew! I had the luck of the Irish — which I am of course.

But the travel left an invisible stain. After the first few years, during an extended absence, homesickness hammered at me. But after getting back, I was itching to be away again within a week. My wife says she always knew when I wanted to go: there would b e a tuneless whistle for a day or two before departure. Even now, at 83 the urge to travel, and always to the old places, is strong. After six months I would go, alone: a trip by plane followed by a train which, strangely, usually ended up in Vienna; which naturally had good connections to Prague and Budapest. In Stephensplatz, the cathedral square, there used to be, certainly in the years up to 1968, the headquarters of the British Council which has over many years done so much to instruct denizens of foreign lands in the British way of life. Not aggressively as the French do, but in a delightful way. P. G. Wodehouse would have been a great local director of the British Council. In Stephensplatz there was the Council's Englische Lesenraum where the English newspapers were available. For me, to be there on a Sunday afternoon reading the Observer, Times and News of the World was a pleasure of high degree. As a variation I sometimes picked up the papers, sauntered the 300 yards down the Kärnterstrasse to Hotel Sacher where I would read them in the comfortable leather chairs provided for the guests who could afford to stay there. The Head Porter knew me by sight, though I never bought even a cup of coffee or a slice of Sacher Torte. May Vienna never change. What other city has the good manners (Küss die Hand, Gnädige Fraulein) , the softening of bad news, the magnificent insincerity, the delightful hypocrisy? You could be in Dublin, except for the good food. But there is a dark side. It is the crossroads between Eastern and Western Europe, and the feeling is more of the East than the West. The cafés since the early 19th century have been the meeting places for dissidents, students of a political bent, and those who were prepared to plot or subvert the governments of the day, which even up to 1945 were less than democratic. The very air, along with the brown coal , smelt of revolt and dissidence.

In Vienna, until she died in 1999, I had a friend, Oda. She was above all things, a wit, sardonic, ironic, yet deeply sympathetic, Viennese, born and educated in Prague but a citizen of Vienna since about 1925. Her mother who died in 1980 at the age of 93 and was herself Viennese born, told me once how she often saw, in the period before 1914, the Emperor Franz Joseph of Austria, Hungary, Bohemia and various parts of what, post 1914, became Yugoslavia, riding down the main road from the Schönbrün Palace three miles outside the centre. He was in a landau carriage, accompanies by his secretary, but no guards, to carry out his duties at the Hofburg, the administrative centre of the empire. So when Oda talked about Vienna it was more "The Third Man" than the "Blue Danube", politics of the between-the-Wars period, and her mother's life under the Emperor. This I listened to in wein stübes, cafés, restaurants that offered other dishes than Wienerschnitzel and, best of all, the last café in Vienna where you could still stay all day for the price of a cup of coffee, a fresh glass of water every half hour and the day's newspapers. The politeness of the 70 year old waiters, with aching feet, was the stuff of legend.

Years move swiftly into decades, and decades into a lifetime, and it is only when you sit and concentrate that the apocalyptic nature of the 50's and 60's is revealed in a mind that was blind to the changes in the human condition while it was happening. Think of the daily work life: 48 hours was the normal week, and plenty thought 56 normal. Everybody worked Saturdays and many welcomed it as it made the afternoon worth waiting for. Football, playing or watching, for the men, the women looking forward to the pub in the evening, the cinema, or both. People were politer and doctors, teachers, policemen and the clergy had not yet lost the public's respect although it was already being replaced with a jocular familiarity. What about shame? Anybody jailed in the 50's would be ostracised after release. Now their neighbours are more likely to throw a street party for them. We are now taught to hate the crime but not the criminal and, indeed, the geneticists tell us that a 'gene' in the victim causes criminal behaviour. Hence he is not responsible for his actions, and we are all to blame. Meaning nobody is to blame. At that point we may just as well black out the word "shame" from the dictionary.

We were a more cohesive people and the focal point of a big town was the professional football club. Its players were mostly born within a few miles of the ground, and the cash nexus had not yet hit the sport. The maximum pay was £10 per week, which was well above the average in-dustrial wage and the lot of every player had he not been a footballer. This kept them more or less in the same social slot as the supporters with whom they were in daily contact, and the bond between both parties and the club was strong. As a result a player might well spend all his playing life with the same club and live in the same neighbourhood.

This intense loyalty was also found in mining villages, dock commu-nities, and wherever bad working conditions brought people together to endure suffering in common. We live in marvellous times now, but what a pity that much that is best in the human condition needed to be sacri-ficed to achieve it.

Perhaps the greatest change to people's lives, then and now, is freedom from the nationalised industries. After 1945 the Socialist Gov-ernment put into public ownership the railways, transport, the steel in-dustry, the mines and health. In 1948 that great act of American generosity, the Marshall Plan, released millions of dollars to European countries and made recovery from the Second World War very swift. Germany, France and Italy used their share to reconstruct their industrial bases, invested in new machine tools and buildings, built up their re-search, design, production, sales and export division, and in the case of Germany, ended exchange control so that the Deutschmark was freely exchanged. The result in a few years was that Europe was booming, alive with industrial activity. Their goods were of high quality and exports boomed. What did we do? We put most of the Marshall Plan money into the nationalised industries which earned nothing, and the NHS which soaked up money like a huge piece of blotting paper. The Europeans, on the other hand, first earned the money and then spent it on the roads, the railways and the health services. And that is why we became poor, with the worst railways and transportation and an NHS which employs more people yet gives the worst patient service in Europe.

For a total of 16 years the people suffered from doctrinal socialism which was already failing in Russia and Eastern Europe. Labour also de-stroyed our marvellous, free grammar schools to replace them with com-prehensives which, among other unpleasant gifts, gave us lower standards and the worst educated labour force in Europe. Nationisation soured and divided people and it implied the customer was always wrong, had an absenteeism of three times that in the private sector, and overmanning of four to one. But everything had to be paid for which is why, for a short time during the Wilson Government, direct taxation for some people reached 98%.

If Mrs. Thatcher had not existed she would have needed to be invented. A woman of conviction politics, of a character and resolution that exceeded that of most of the men in her Cabinet, she was not loved but, more importantly, was respected and did what had to be done. She broke the power of the Unions, denationalised the mines and tamed their leaders, denationalised steel, post office telephones, transport and the public utilities. As an example, in 1978 the steel industry produced 25 million tons with 270,000 people. By 1981 they were making 19,000,000 tons with 60,000 people and it was the best quality and the cheapest in Europe. That is what happens when the people are set free. But even Thatcher flinched from dealing with the NHS, which needed a root and branch attack on waste, inefficiency, overmanning in bureaucrats, supernumiraries, undermanning in nurses and doctors, and appalling patient waiting lists. The trouble was, at that time (1988 – 1990), the NHS was such a national icon that the country still thought we had the best health service in Europe instead of the worst. Now, 13 years later, it is even worse.

The people were at last free, to work where they wanted, to buy what they wanted, to write what they wanted, to travel where they wanted, and to be respected throughout the world. And, let us not forget, to have a telephone installed in 24 hours instead of 6 months.

I recall an amusing, though serious, commentary on the difference between the freedom of capitalism and the imprisonment of dictatorial regimes, it was:

Socialism is when you have two cows and give one to your neighbour.
Communism is when you have two cows and the State takes both and gives you milk.
Fascism is when you have two cows and the State takes both and sells you milk.
Nazism is when you have two cows and the State takes both and shoots you.

Capitalism is when you have two cows, sell one and buy a bull.
Bureaucracy is when you have two cows and the State takes both, shoots one,
   milks the other and pours the milk down the drain."

As to the accuracy of Communist practice, I was in Moscow sometime in 1958 for several weeks. Suddenly, without explanation, there was
no milk. It was normal to have no oranges, no lemons, no vegetables, no
brown shoes in the shops as well as black ones, and the Moscovites learnt
to live with these shortages, but no milk? After several days there was still
no milk but plenty of yoghurt. The milk had been 'lost' somewhere en
route to Moscow, sour of course, when found, so the bureaucrats turned
it into yoghurt. You couldn't make it up.

I shall now write about confidence. You can't touch it, feel it, smell it
or taste it, but without it no man or woman can lead a political party to
victory, nobody can create a company and make it profitable, no general
can win a war and, of course, not to neglect the other side of the coin, a
would-be conman without it couldn't sell Tower Bridge to a trusting
American.

The greatest exercise in confidence is probably that shown by a small
child who asks a man to hold her hand while crossing a busy road. It
would be a brave man who would do that today, lest the good deed be
observed by a policeman or, worse, a female social worker, and he was ar-
rested 'bang to rights' as a filthy, evil paedophile. Nevertheless, such confidence given by a child is a wonderful thing, full of hope for the future
and faith in the past. Confidence is something immeasurable, untouchable, unmatchable, an invisible glue that binds a man to a friend, a wife to
his job and a soldier to his comrades. Now, how can I best describe it?
There are three stories that I have treasured over the years. One is an
Aesop's Fable, the second is from an American television comedy, and the
third is true, as I know the people in it.

Let us call the first, "Confidence Misplaced".

There was a fire in the forest and all the animals, big and small,
mammals, reptiles and insects trying to escape fled towards the nearby
river. A frog and a scorpion arrived on the river bank together and the
scorpion said to the frog, "Will you take me over the river on your back

as I cannot swim?" "But", said the frog, "if I do you will sting me and we will both drown". "No! No! said the scorpion, "I promise not to sting you". "Well", said the frog, "I'm not sure, but if I don't help you who else will?" So the scorpion clambered on the frog's back and they set off. Halfway across the scorpion stung the frog who cried out and said "There! I told you so and now we will both drown! Why did you do it?" "Because," said the scorpion, "It's my nature."

And the second, "Confidence Gone Mad".

A feature of the American TV show "Bilko" was that its star character, Sergeant Bilko, a betting man, always won his bet against the odds. One day his platoon cook, Rupert, confided that he had been born in Nebraska. "Not so," said Bilko, "you were born in Tokyo, and I'll bet you 50 dollars on that." "Done," said Rupert, "I know I was born in Nebraska and I'll ask my mother , to prove it." Which he did. And came back triumphantly to collect his winnings. "Told you so," he said, "My Ma said I was born in Nebraska." "No you weren't." said Bilko, "She's in denial for some reason, maybe she should see a doctor." At which point Rupert gets anxious. "Do you think so? Should I tell her?" "No," said Bilko, "She'd only get worse with the worry, and what the hell, Tokyo or Nebraska, I'm your platoon Sergeant, and it was Tokyo all right. Trust me, I always look after my men." A crestfallen Rupert said "Thank you, Bilko, I'm glad you put my mind at rest." and he paid up. Now confidence like that takes some beating.

Now, the third I call "Confidence Triumphant".

In the less turbulent days of the mid 60's there was a young man, an engineer and brilliant entrepreneur who had built a company to produce a component for sale in the car industry, and it was already achieving respectable sales. But to increase its sales four or five fold, he required such capital as could only be found in the City of London to finance building, construction, machine tools, labour etc. He was given the name of a merchant banker, highly respected and of great experience. He made the contact, and went to the offices of this banker. He was warmly welcomed by a handsome grey haired gent formally clad in the regulation pin striped suit, blue striped shirt and old Etonian tie, who listened carefully and put many questions as the young man told the tale. "You simply must get the finance as the idea is sound and the danger of failure is small. At present my bank is stretched to breaking point and it would be at least a year before we could help. But I'll tell you what we can do. It's a fine day, let us walk a while outside in the sun and talk about it further." So he took the young man's arm and together they sauntered up and down the pavement in full sight of the City's great and the good. Next day he received two phone calls. Both were similar and said "I saw you yesterday talking with Mr. —————, an old friend of my company, and I wondered what might be in the wind so I rang him. Perhaps we can get together and talk." The young man got his finance. Now, that is confidence, whose value is beyond price.

Most after dinner speeches tend to be turgid, long, and sometimes downright embarrassing. These three stories tell you just about all you need to know about life and are a complete speech without the need to say more. Read them, learn, and inwardly digest. Which, I think, was good advice offered by the 16th century Francis Bacon.

As to the rest of my life, a few more trips, the occasional luncheon in London, preceded by a drink at the Coach and Horses in Greek Street, hoping to bump into the ghost of Jeffrey Barnard. A saunter down Jermyn Street to look at the expensive shirts in Turnbull and Asser. And do most of the other things I have been doing these many years as well. I've had a damn good life but am not yet ready, like Simeon, to ask for my nunc dimitus.

The dogs bark, and the caravan moves on.

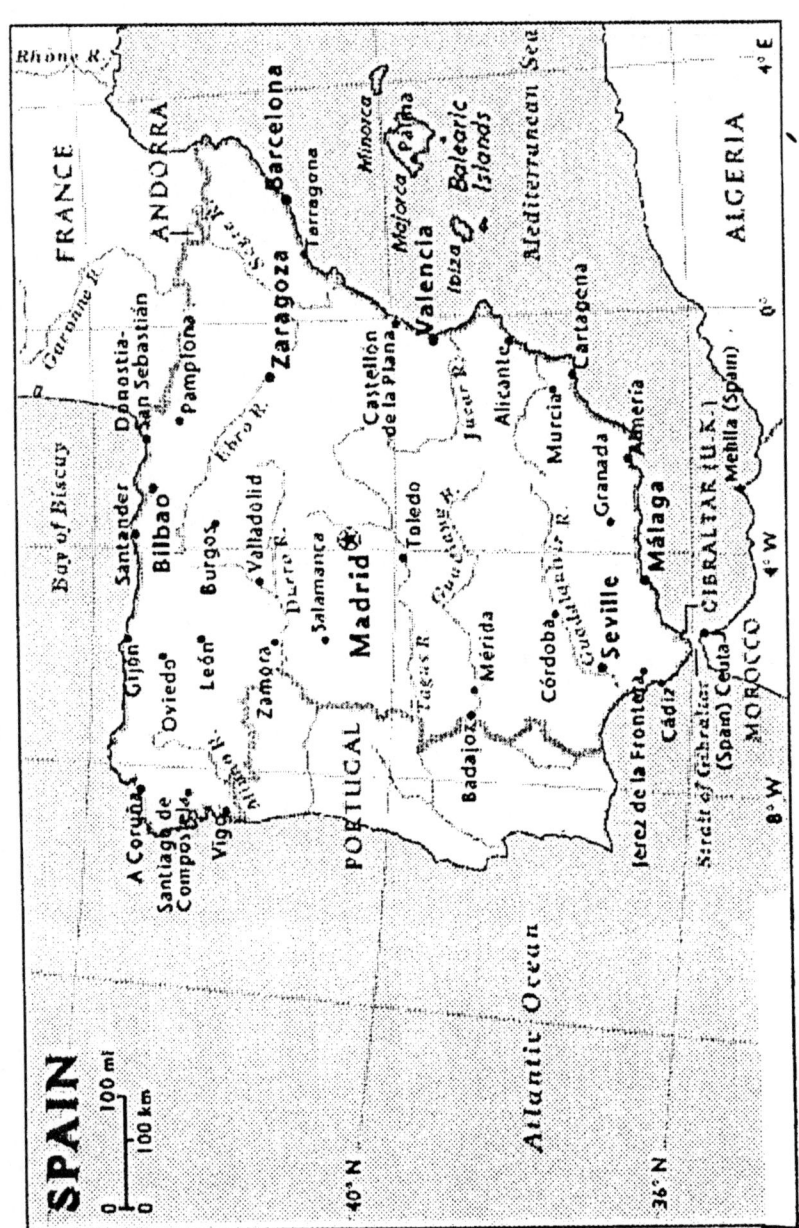

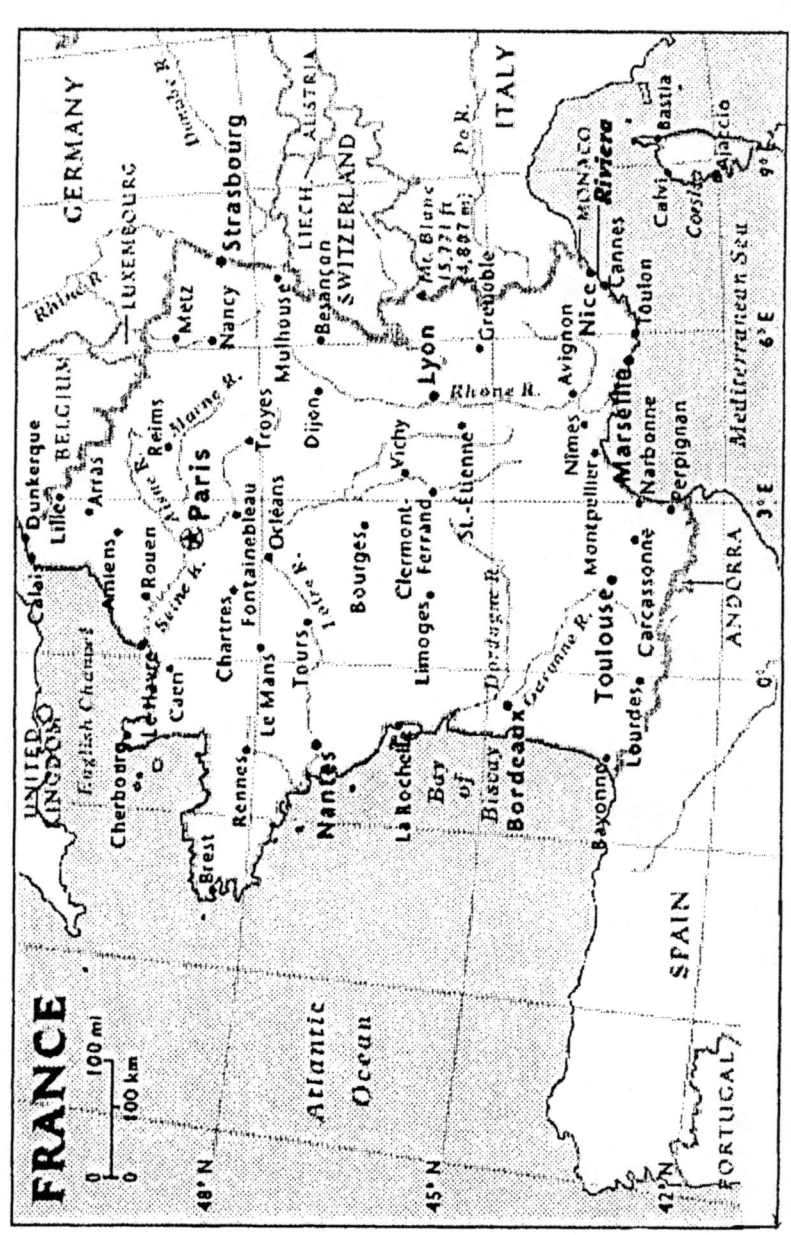

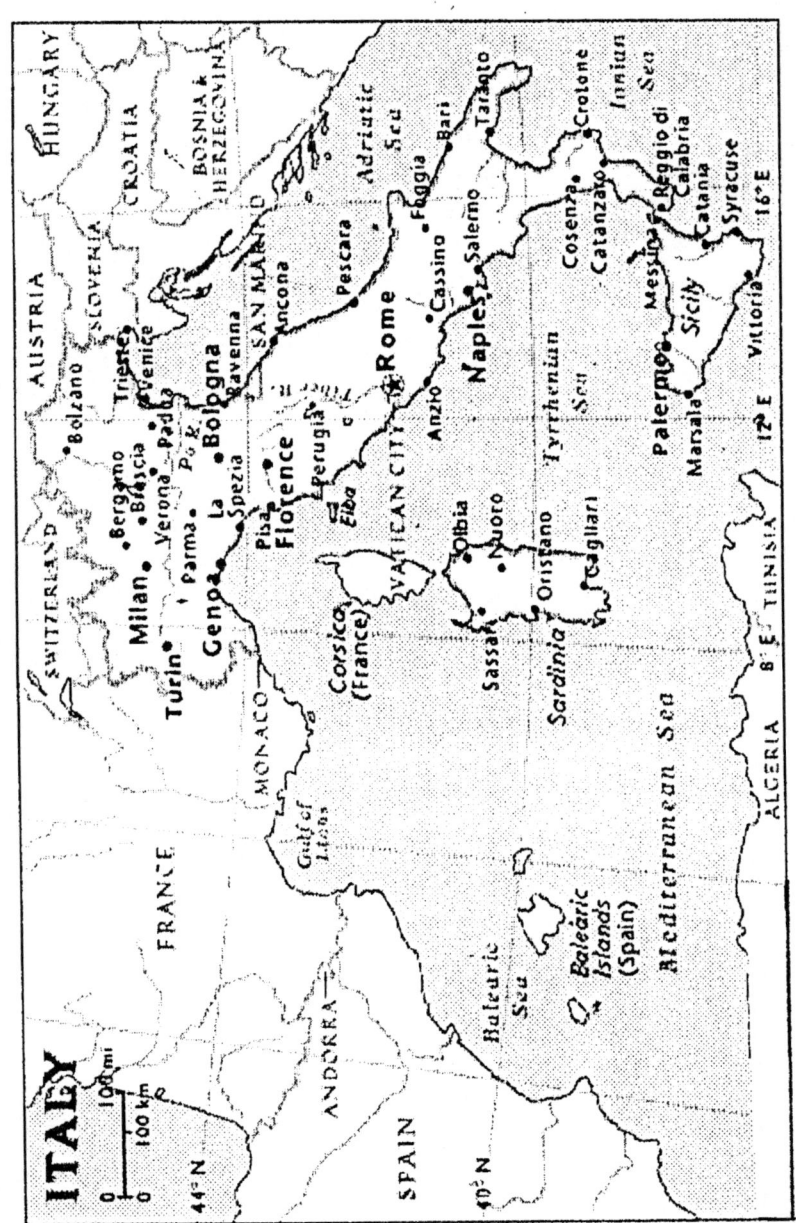

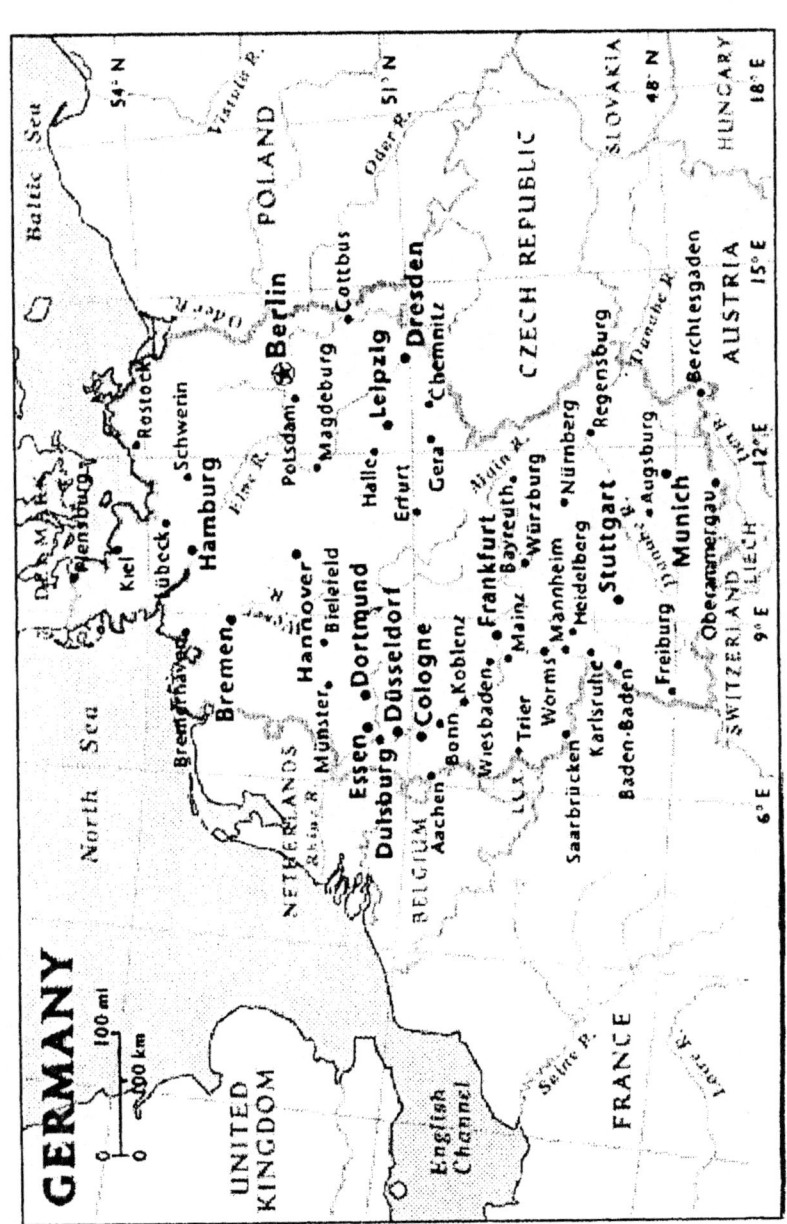

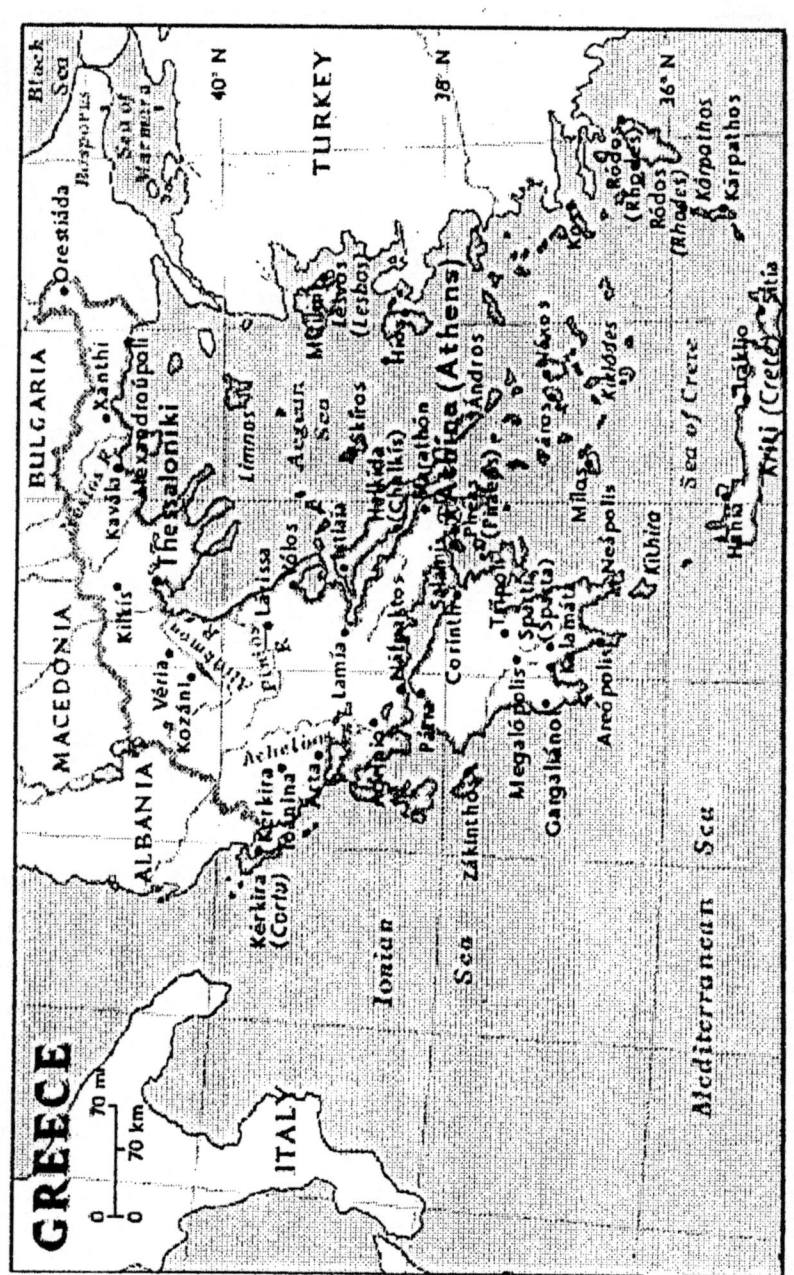

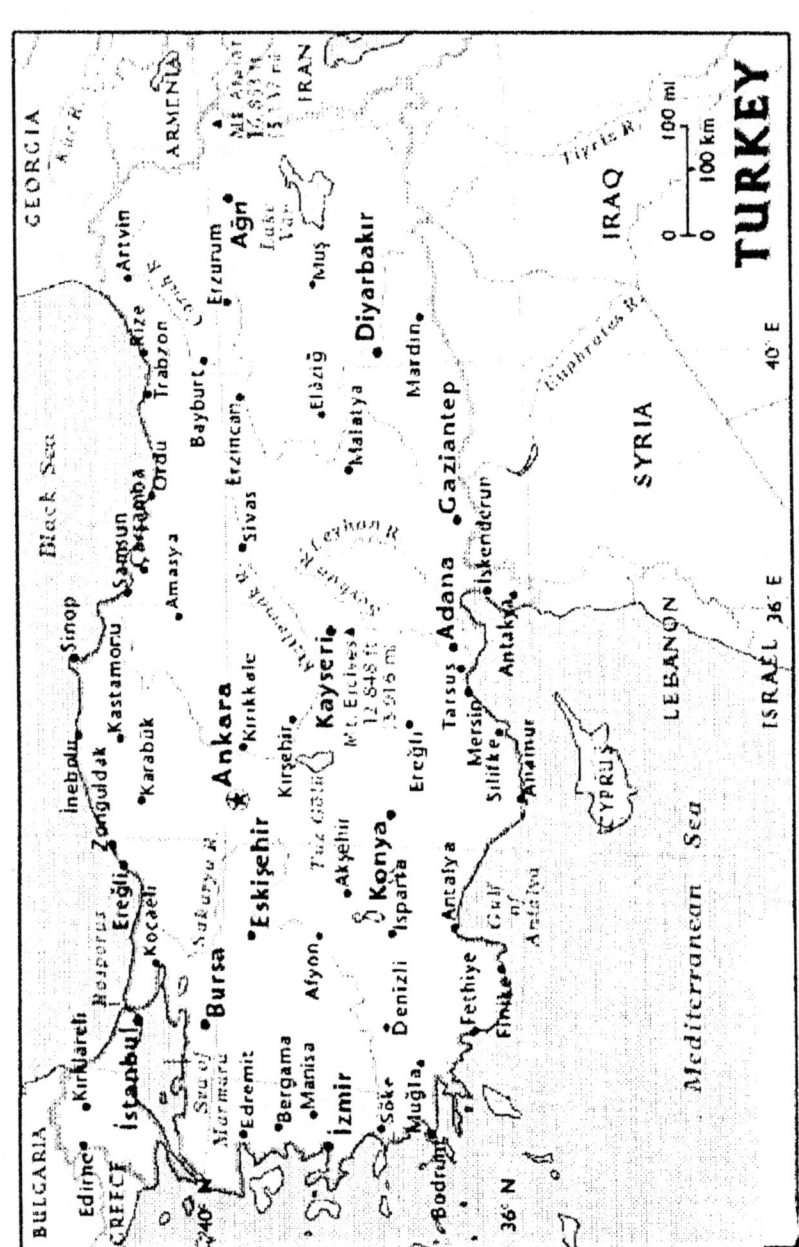

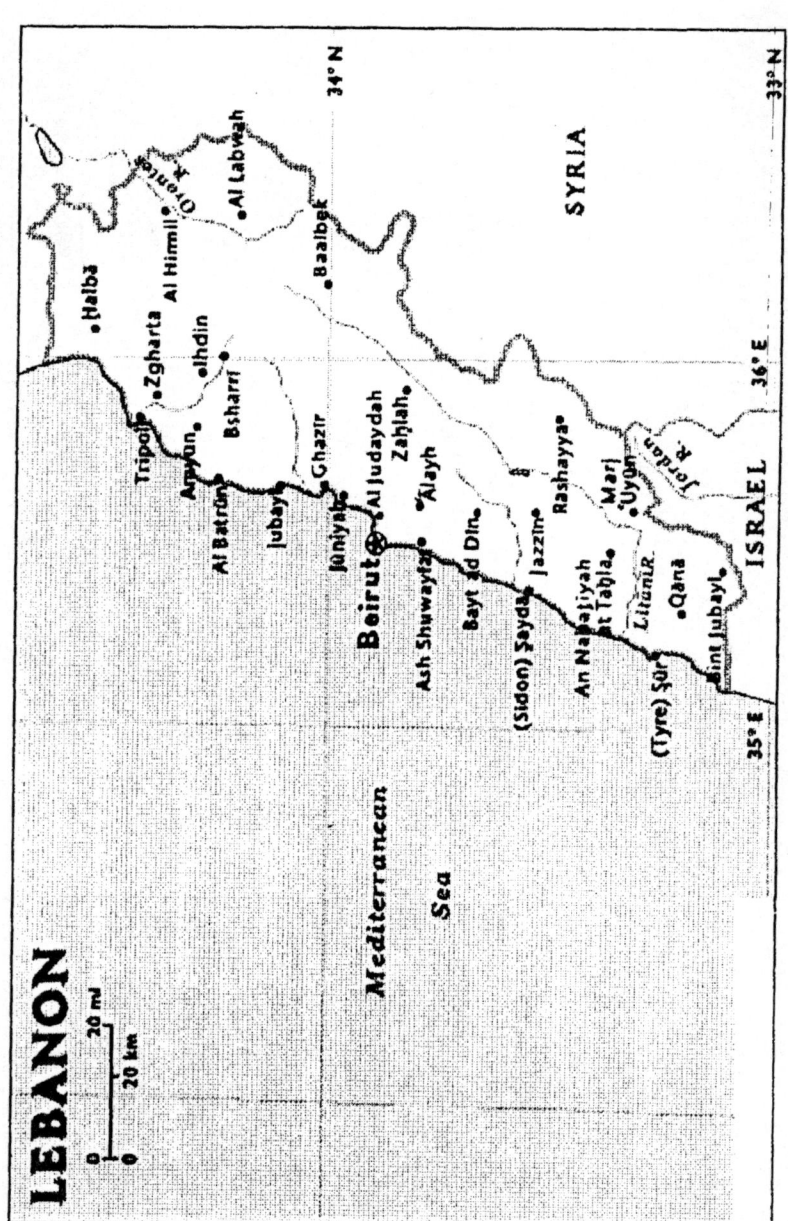

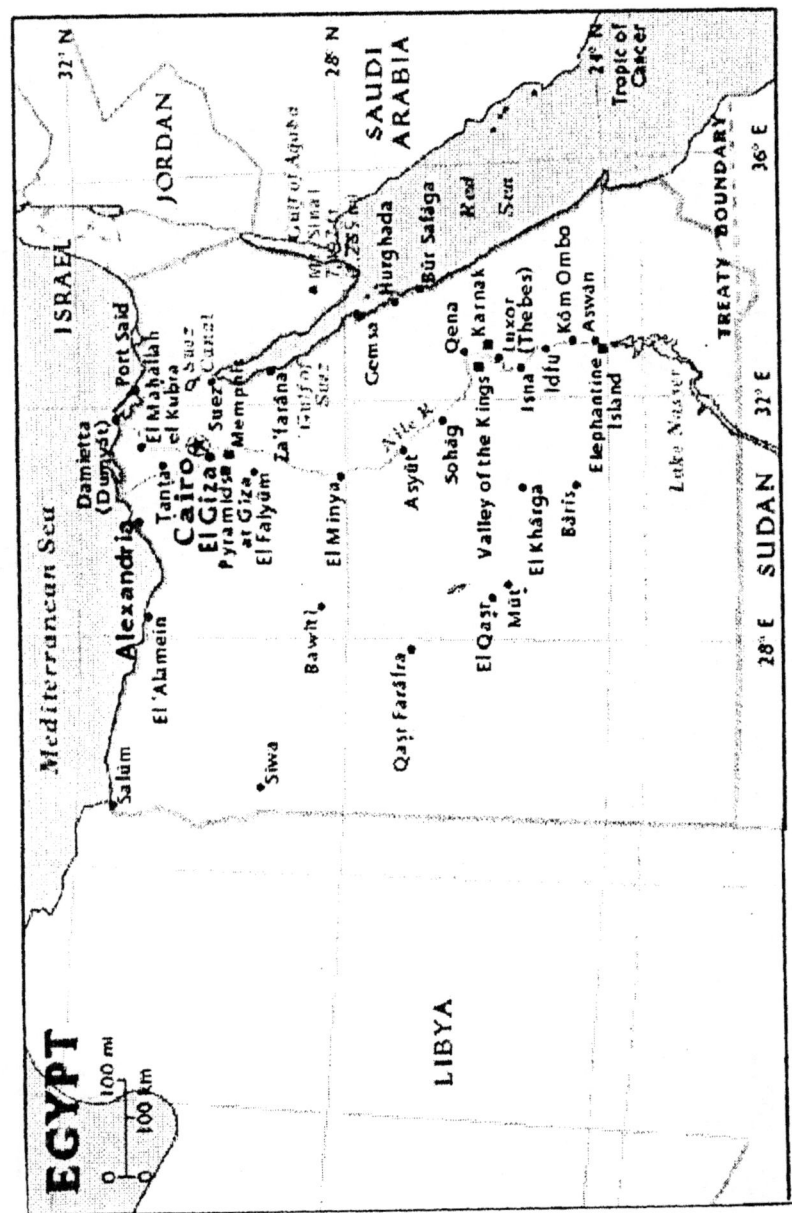

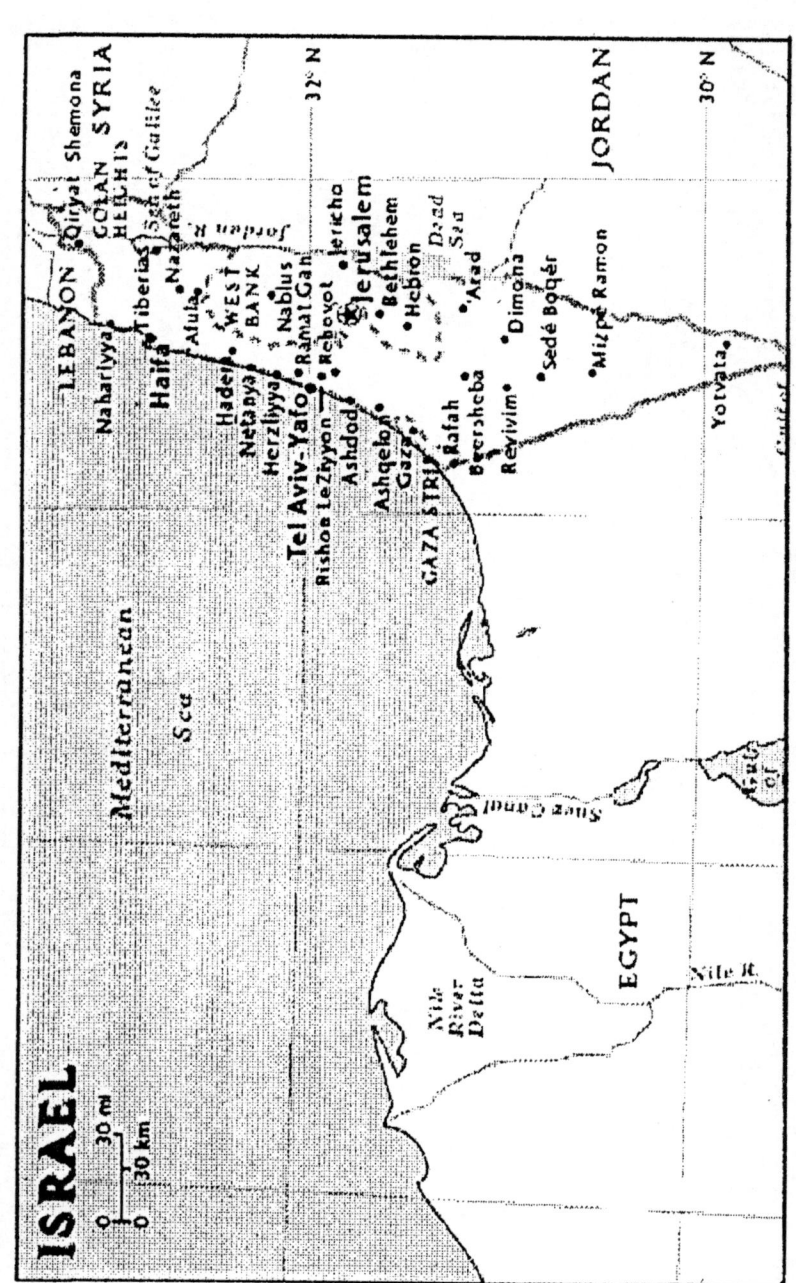

ISRAEL

LEBANON
SYRIA
GOLAN HEIGHTS
JORDAN
EGYPT
Mediterranean Sea

Qiryat Shemona
Nahariyya
Haifa
Tiberias
Sea of Galilee
Nazareth
Afula
Hadera
Netanya
Herzliyya
Tel Aviv-Yafo
Rishon LeZiyyon
Ashdod
Ashqelon
Gaza
GAZA STRIP
Rafah
Rishon LeZiyyon
Ramat Gan
WEST BANK
Nablus
Jordan R.
Jericho
Jerusalem
Bethlehem
Hebron
Dead Sea
Arad
Dimona
Sedé Boqér
Mizpé Ramon
Beersheba
Revivim
Yotvata

Nile River Delta
Suez Canal
Nile R.

0   30 mi
0   30 km

32° N
30° N

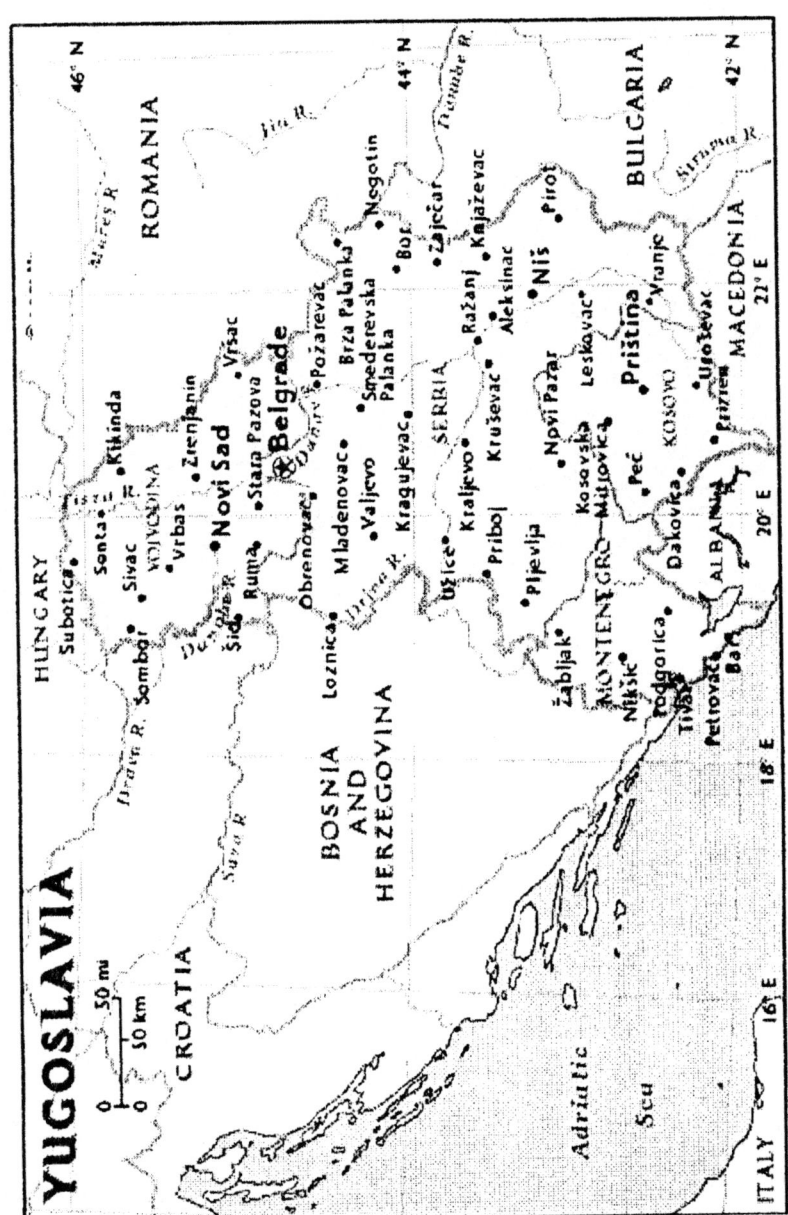

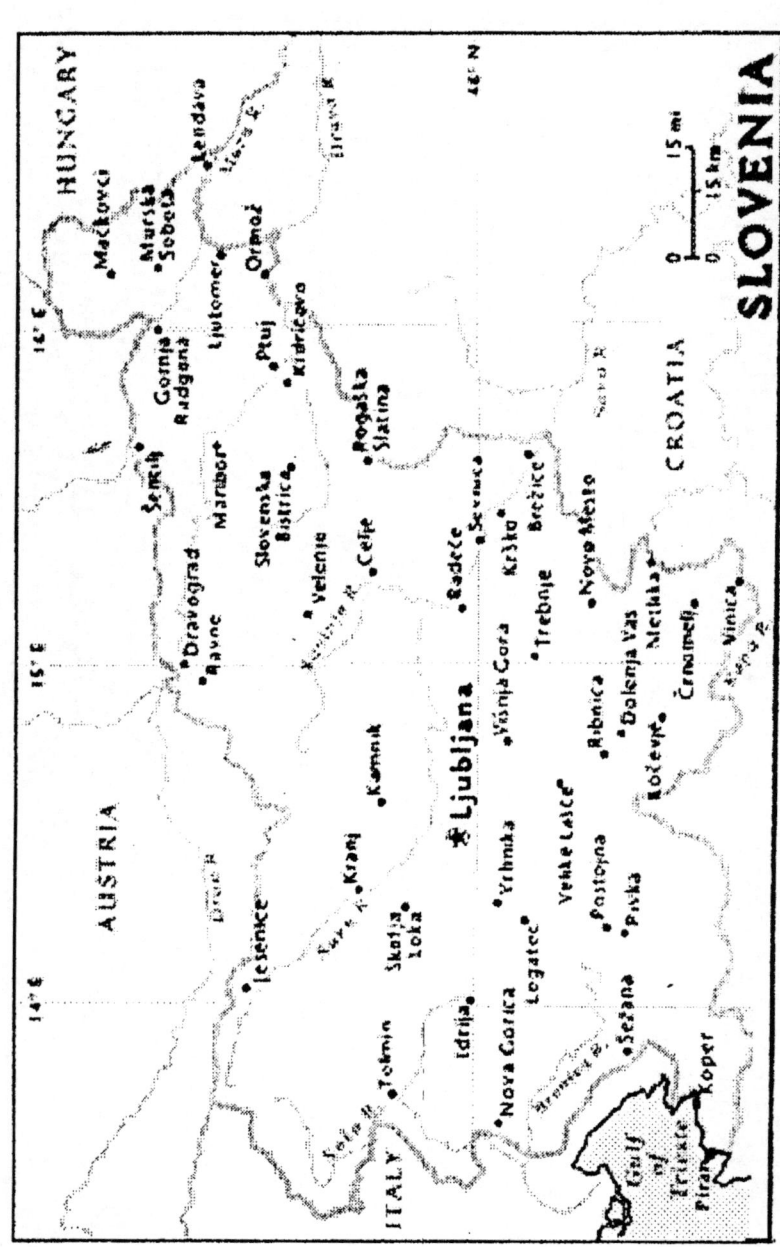

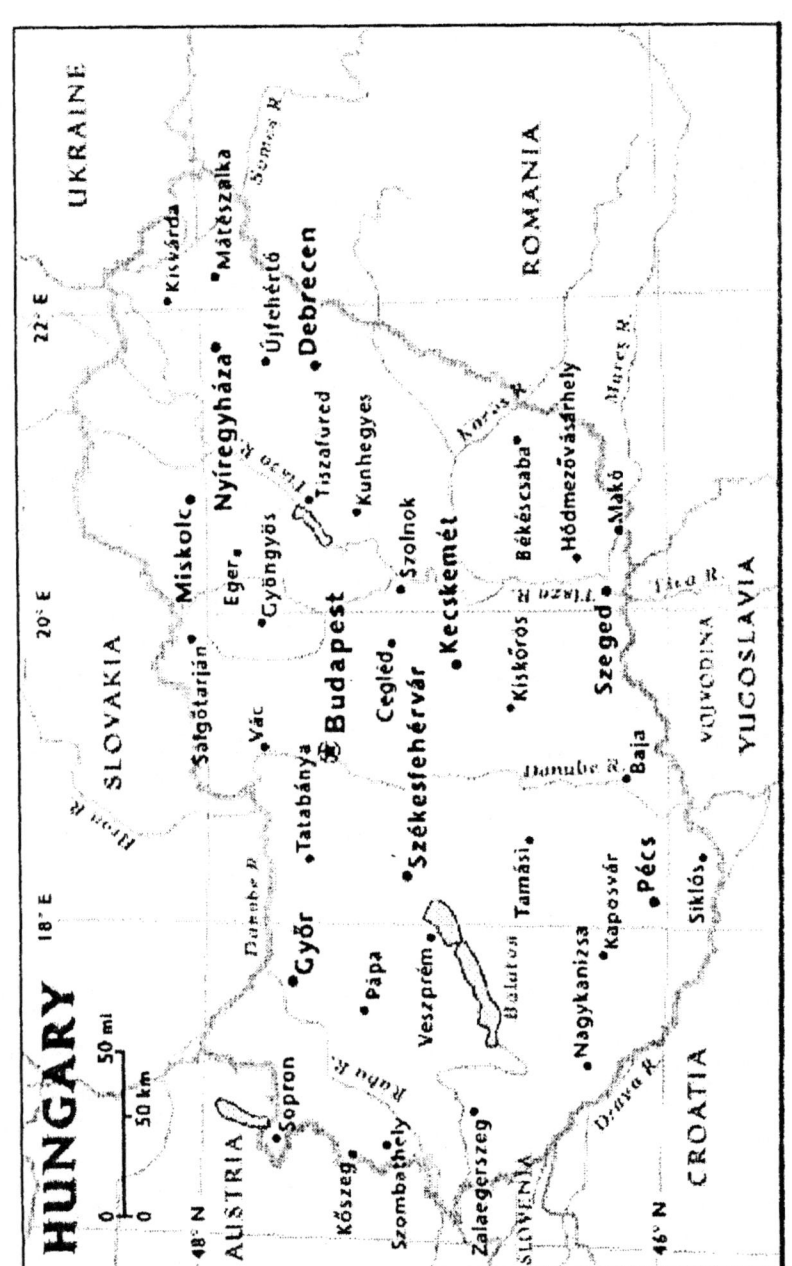

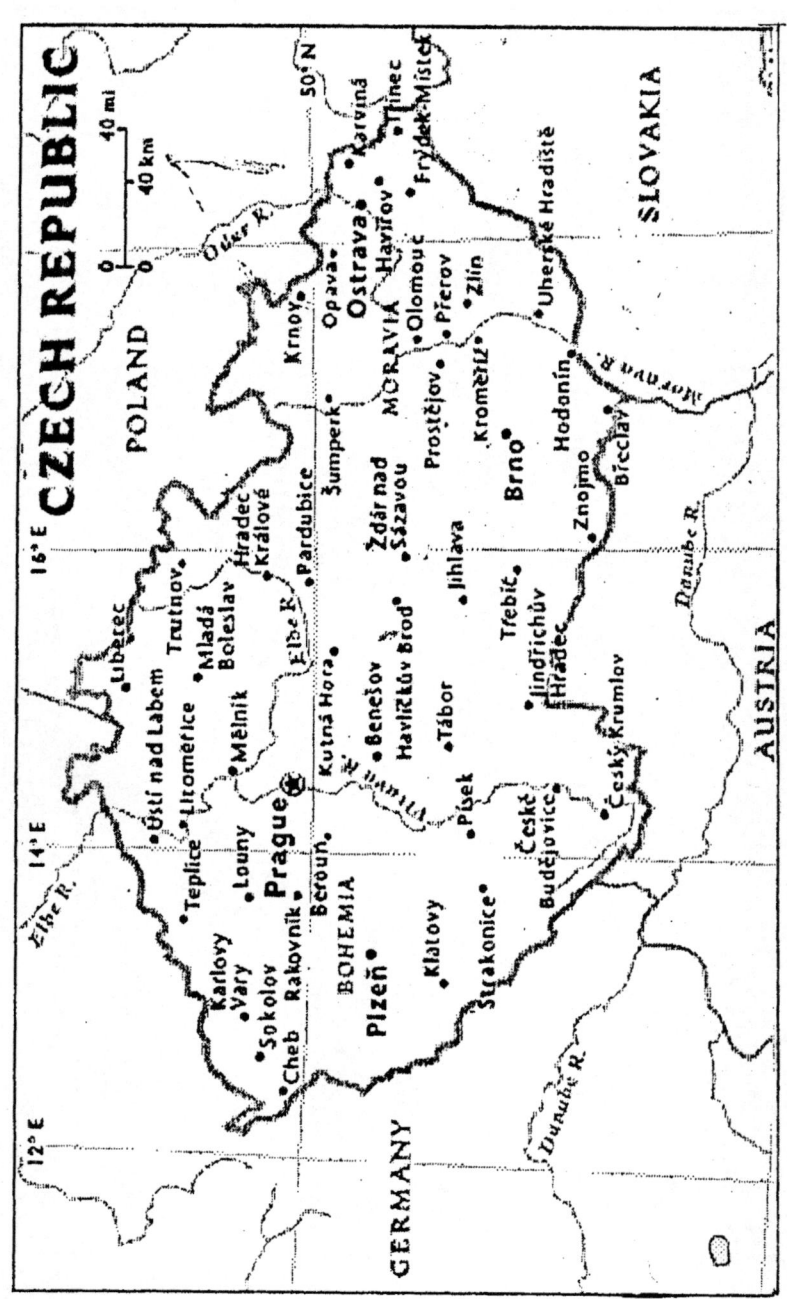